THE POWER
OF NATURE

USBORNE SCIENCE & EXPERIMENTS

THE POWER
OF NATURE

SCHOLASTIC INC.
ew York Toronto London Auckland Sydney

ISBN 0-590-92188-6

"Energy and Power" copyright © 1990 by Usborne Publishing Ltd.
"Weather and Climate" copyright © 1992 by Usborne Publishing Ltd.
All rights reserved. Published by Scholastic Inc., 555 Broadway, New York,
NY 10012, by arrangement with Usborne Publishing Ltd.

12 11 10 9 8 7 6 5 4 3 2   7 8 9/9 0 1 2/0

Printed in the U.S.A.   09

First Scholastic printing, April 1997

CONTENTS

Book One   Weather & Climate   Page 1

Book Two   Energy & Power   Page 49

USBORNE SCIENCE & EXPERIMENTS

THE POWER OF NATURE

BOOK ONE
WEATHER & CLIMATE

Fiona Watt and Francis Wilson, Television Weatherman

Edited by Corinne Stockley

Designed by Paul Greenleaf

Illustrated by Kuo Kang Chen, Peter Dennis and Denise Finney

Additional designs by Stephen Wright

Contents

3   About this book
4   Planetary weather
6   Heating the Earth
8   Pressure and winds
10 Moving air
12 Clouds
14 Water in the air
16 Highs, lows and fronts
18 Thunderstorms and hurricanes
20 Extreme weather conditions
22 Local weather
24 Monitoring the weather
26 Your own weather station
28 Analyzing information
30 Weather forecasts
32 Worldwide climate
34 People and climate
36 Changing climates
38 Present-day climate changes
40 Pollution in the atmosphere
42 Predicting future weather
44 Record weather extremes
46 Glossary
48 Index

USBORNE SCIENCE & EXPERIMENTS

About this book

From pleasant sunny days to devastating storms, the weather is part of daily life for everyone in the world. This book explains how many of the different elements of the atmosphere combine to produce different types of weather. It also describes how different weather conditions produce the wide variety of climates which are found throughout the world.

The book examines the ways in which the weather is monitored all over the world, and the processes involved in gathering information in order to make accurate forecasts. It explores how climates have changed since the Earth was first formed, and what effect current environmental problems may have on the atmosphere, weather and climates in the future.

Activities and projects

Special boxes like this one are used throughout the book for activities, projects and experiments. They will help you to understand the principles of different kinds of weather and its formation. You should be able to find most of the necessary equipment at home, but you may need to go to a hardware shop to buy a few of the items.

Using the glossary

The glossary on pages 46-47 is a useful reference point. It gives detailed explanations of the more complex terms used in the book, as well as introducing some new words.

This scene shows a tropical cyclone, or hurricane. Hurricane winds can cause serious damage to buildings and trees and also create gigantic waves which crash onto shores. To find out more about hurricanes and how they are formed, see pages 18-19.

Planetary weather

The Earth is one of a group of planets which make up the Solar System. Each planet is surrounded by a mixture of different gases which is called its atmosphere. The weather on each planet depends on its distance from the Sun and the movements of the gases in its atmosphere.

The Sun's radiation

The Sun's radiation is made up of rays of different strengths of energy. Relatively speaking, they are all high energy rays but some are stronger than others. Some of these rays give us light, and they all heat up anything which absorbs them. Certain gases in the thermosphere and ozone in the stratosphere (see page 5) absorb some of the highest energy radiation (which is harmful). Clouds also absorb or reflect some of it. However, most of the Sun's radiation reaches the Earth's surface,

where it is absorbed by the land or sea, or is reflected.

As it absorbs high energy radiation, the Earth warms up, and sends out lower energy radiation into the atmosphere. Some of this radiation escapes into space, but some is absorbed by gases in the atmosphere, such as carbon dioxide. These gases then send out slightly lower energy radiation in all directions. Some of this reaches the Earth's surface where it is absorbed and again heats the surface.

High energy radiation from the Sun (solar radiation).

Most harmful radiation is absorbed by gases in the thermosphere and stratosphere (see page 5).

Some radiation is absorbed by, or reflected from clouds. Some is reflected from the Earth's surface (see page 7).

The warmed Earth gives off lower energy radiation. Some is absorbed by gases in the lowest layer of atmosphere.

These gases send out radiation in all directions.

Most of the high energy solar radiation is absorbed by the Earth's surface, which is heated.

Earth's surface

Some radiation returns to the Earth's surface which again absorbs it and is heated.

The Sun

The Sun sends out energy in the form of rays of heat and light called radiation. The amount of heat and light energy which reaches the planets in the Solar System depends on their distance from the Sun.

Mercury

Weather on different planets

Scientists have used information from space probes to work out what the weather may be like on other planets. The atmosphere of each planet in the Solar System is held to the planet by gravity and pushes down on its surface. This is called atmospheric pressure (known as air pressure on Earth). The planets have different atmospheric gases and pressures, which greatly affect the weather found on each one. The examples below are the planets nearest to the Earth.

Venus

Weather on Venus

On Venus, the atmosphere is very dense, with pressure over 90 times greater than on Earth. The planet's atmosphere is mainly made up of carbon dioxide, which is very good at trapping heat. This makes temperatures as high as 887°F.

The Earth takes about 24 hours (a day) to rotate all the way round once.

Venus takes 243 Earth days to rotate.

Venus is surrounded by thick clouds containing droplets of sulphuric acid. These droplets may sometimes fall as rain, but they evaporate before reaching the ground and form clouds again. There are also continuous lightning storms.

The Earth

The Moon

The Moon

The Moon is not a planet, but a satellite of the Earth. A satellite is any object in space which travels around, or orbits, a larger object such as a planet. Other moons orbit other planets. Mars, for instance, has two moons, and Jupiter has sixteen.

There is no water, wind and weather on the Moon, and it is covered with dust. There is also no atmosphere surrounding it, because the Moon's force of gravity is so weak that any gases cannot be held to its surface.

Mars

The atmosphere on Mars is very thin with very low pressure. It is mainly made up of carbon dioxide with some nitrogen. There is no water on the surface, but there are areas of ice at the north and south poles. Temperatures are very low: −20°F during the day, falling to −121°F at night.

From Mars, the sky appears to be pink. This is caused by dust from the red, rocky surface being blown into the air by strong winds.

Jupiter

Jupiter's atmosphere appears to be a mass of swirling gases, which surround a solid center, or core. The gases are thought to be hydrogen and helium. Temperatures on the planet are thought to be very low, not rising above −200°F.

The Great Red Spot on the surface of Jupiter's atmosphere is thought to be a massive storm.

The Earth's atmosphere

The Earth's atmosphere is divided into layers (see below) according to temperature, although there are no solid boundaries separating each layer. The Earth is the only planet in the Solar System which has large amounts of water, both in its atmosphere, and on or below its surface.

The magnetosphere is the uppermost layer. It contains no gases, but forms a barrier which stops many particles from space entering the Earth's atmosphere. Most weather satellites (see page 25) are found way up beyond this layer.

The air in the exosphere is extremely thin as it contains very few gases. The top of this layer is about 560 miles from the ground. Some polar orbiting weather satellites (see page 25) are found in this layer.

The thermosphere contains gases that absorb some of the harmful solar radiation, and so heat up this layer. The temperature at the top, which is about 280 miles from the ground, may be as high as 3,632°F, but it decreases as you go down.

The mesosphere reaches a height of about 50 miles. It is coldest at the top, about -148°F, but warms up towards the bottom because of the warmer stratosphere below.

The top of the stratosphere is about 31 miles from the ground. Ozone gas forms a separate layer within it. This absorbs some of the Sun's harmful rays, heating up the layer. The temperature is highest at the top, about 32°F, cooling down towards the troposphere below. Jet aircraft fly here, where the air is still, or stable.

The troposphere varies in height between 6 miles and 12 miles. Its lowest temperature is at the top, about -58°F, but the air warms up the nearer you get to the surface. All the things that combine to make our weather are found in this layer.

Earth's surface

5

Heating the Earth

The way that the Sun's rays strike the surface of the Earth is important in determining the temperature of an area. In turn, the amount of heat received by any given area has a direct influence on the weather, as it affects the temperature of the air lying immediately above it.

The Sun's heat and the seasons

Not all places on the Earth's surface receive the same amount of heat from the Sun. The Earth is tilted at an angle, and its surface is curved, so the parallel rays of the Sun strike some areas full on, and others at more oblique angles.

As the Earth travels around the Sun in its orbit, the effect of its tilt is gradually to change the area which receives the most direct heat. At the start of each orbit, one hemisphere is tilted towards the Sun. After half the orbit (6 months later), the opposite hemisphere is in that position. The change in temperature due to this effect causes the seasons.

Near the equator, the seasons do not have great differences in temperature. The Sun's rays strike almost full-on all year round, so the temperature remains high.

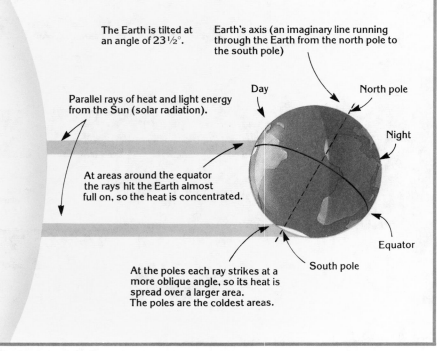

The Earth is tilted at an angle of 23½°.

Earth's axis (an imaginary line running through the Earth from the north pole to the south pole)

Parallel rays of heat and light energy from the Sun (solar radiation).

Day

North pole

Night

At areas around the equator the rays hit the Earth almost full on, so the heat is concentrated.

Equator

At the poles each ray strikes at a more oblique angle, so its heat is spread over a larger area. The poles are the coldest areas.

South pole

The further away from the equator a place is, the lower its summer and winter temperatures in comparison with places at the equator.

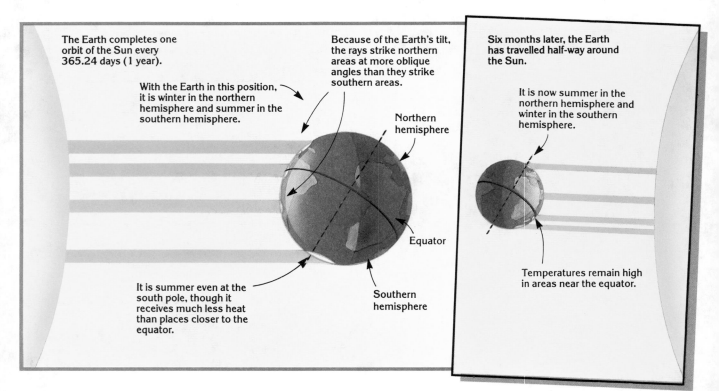

The Earth completes one orbit of the Sun every 365.24 days (1 year).

With the Earth in this position, it is winter in the northern hemisphere and summer in the southern hemisphere.

Because of the Earth's tilt, the rays strike northern areas at more oblique angles than they strike southern areas.

Northern hemisphere

Equator

It is summer even at the south pole, though it receives much less heat than places closer to the equator.

Southern hemisphere

Six months later, the Earth has travelled half-way around the Sun.

It is now summer in the northern hemisphere and winter in the southern hemisphere.

Temperatures remain high in areas near the equator.

Surface temperatures

As well as some places receiving more solar radiation than others, there are also differences in the amount of this radiation which is absorbed by different surfaces. Forests, sand and bare soil absorb more radiation than surfaces such as snow and ice, which reflect most of it. The temperature of the air in contact with a surface depends on the temperature of that surface.

Bare soil, such as a plowed field, absorbs a large amount of radiation, heating the surface.

Snow and ice absorb very little solar radiation. Most of it is reflected into the atmosphere.

Air temperatures remain low.

A bottle fountain

A bottle fountain shows how heated air expands. To make one, you will need a glass bottle with a plastic screw-top, a corkscrew, some food colouring, a straw, some sticky putty* and a needle.

What to do

1. Make a hole in the ▶ bottle top using a corkscrew (be careful with the sharp point).

Corkscrew

Bottle top

The hole must be big enough for the straw to fit through.

Food colouring

Bottle

Water

◀ 2. Half fill the bottle with cold water. Add a few drops of food coloring.

Needle

Hole

Sticky putty

Bottle

Straw

Make sure the end is in the water.

3. Screw the top tightly onto ▶ the bottle. Push the straw through the hole and seal around it with some sticky putty. Make a plug of sticky putty in the top of the straw. Use a needle to pierce a hole down through the plug.

Fountain

Hot water

Air pressure

◀ 4. Carefully put the bottle in a deep bowl of very hot water. As the air in the bottle is heated, it expands and pushes down on the water, forcing water out of the straw.

Air temperatures

The Earth's surface is mainly heated by the absorption of solar radiation (see page 4). Where areas of the surface are warmer than the layer of air immediately above them, this air is heated.

Warmed air expands, becomes less dense and rises. Surrounding cooler air moves in to replace the rising warm air. The warm air cools as it rises, becomes denser again and eventually stops rising. It sinks back to Earth, where it may be heated again if the surface is still warmer than the air above. This circulation of warm and cold currents of air is called convection, and the currents are convection currents.

Air in contact with the surface is heated.

This air is less dense than the surrounding air, expands and rises.

Surrounding cooler air moves in to take its place.

Warm air eventually cools and sinks.

The particles in warm air move around rapidly and are less densely packed.

Rising current of warm air (thermal)

The particles in cool air move more slowly and are closer together, so this air is more dense.

Earth's surface

Convection currents can occur over large areas of the Earth's surface, where large masses of air are heated from below. They can also occur above a small, surface area, such as above a newly-ploughed field. The currents of rising warm air are called thermals.

* Sticky putty is used for sticking paper or posters to walls.

Pressure and winds

The pressure of the air on the Earth's surface is different in different places. This is partly due to the different amounts of heat they receive. Pressure differences cause the movement of air (winds).

Air pressure also decreases with altitude (height above sea level), because there is a greater amount of air pushing down on the surface at sea level than higher up, for instance on a mountain.

Differences in air pressure

When air rises, it leaves behind an area of lower pressure, because the upward-moving air is not pressing down so hard on the surface. Areas of high pressure are formed where air is sinking back down, and so pushing down harder.

If a pressure difference exists, air moves from the higher to the lower pressure area, in order to even out the pressure.

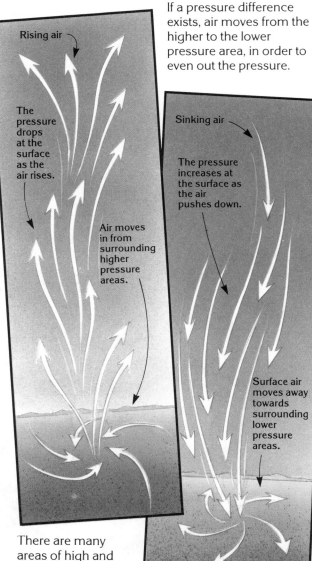

Rising air

The pressure drops at the surface as the air rises.

Air moves in from surrounding higher pressure areas.

Sinking air

The pressure increases at the surface as the air pushes down.

Surface air moves away towards surrounding lower pressure areas.

There are many areas of high and low pressure above the Earth's surface, due to such things as uneven surface heating. Air moves between these, forming surface winds.

Measuring air pressure

Air pressure is measured in millibars* on a barometer. You can make a model barometer using a large, narrow, plastic bottle, two rubber bands, some cardboard and some water.

What to do

1. Cut a 1 in strip of thin cardboard and draw a scale along one edge. Attach the cardboard to the bottle using the rubber bands.

Bottle

Thin cardboard

Rubber bands

Scale

2. Fill the bottle with water so it is three quarters full. Also fill the bowl nearly to the top with water.

Try not to get the scale wet

Bottle

Bowl   Water

3. Place your hand over the top of the bottle and turn it upside-down. Put your hand into the bowl so that the neck of the bottle is under the water. Remove your hand from under the bottle and stand it in the bowl.

Turn the bottle over carefully.

Try not to let any water out.

Bottle   Water

Bowl

4. The water level in the bottle will rise and fall with the air pressure, as more or less air pushes down on the water in the bowl.

Mark the water level on the day you make your barometer (you could find out what the air pressure is, and write this too).

Major pressure areas of the world

Around the Earth there are several major bands where high or low pressure predominates (although in each band individual areas of different pressure may occur – see page 10). There is a general pattern of air movement from the high pressure to the low pressure areas.

The Earth's surface receives the most solar radiation around the equator. The land greatly heats up the air immediately above it, and this vast amount of air rises, leaving a band of predominately low pressure, called the Intertropical Convergence Zone (ITCZ), at the surface. This sets up all other air movements.

The warm air rising above the equator spreads out and cools, sinking around latitudes 30° north and south of the equator. The sinking air pushes down on the surface, creating a band of high pressure, so when it reaches the surface, the air moves north and south towards areas of lower pressure.

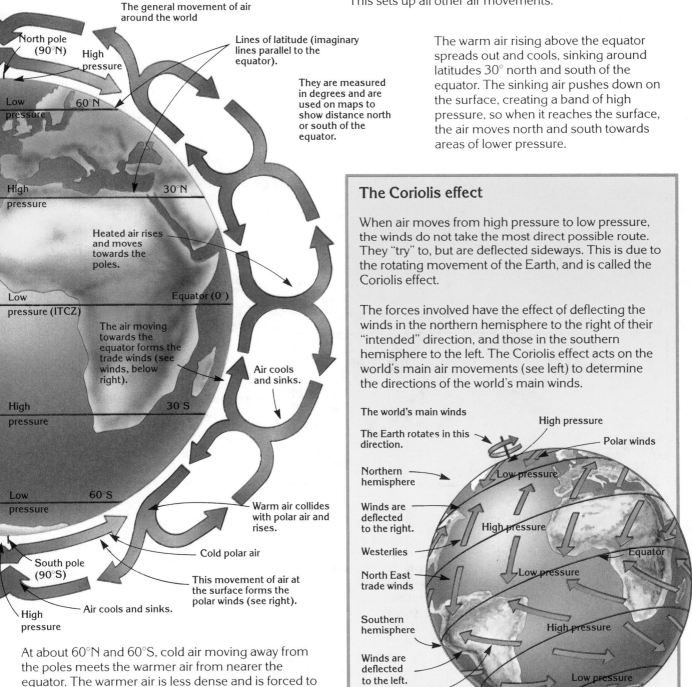

The general movement of air around the world

North pole (90°N)

High pressure

Lines of latitude (imaginary lines parallel to the equator).

They are measured in degrees and are used on maps to show distance north or south of the equator.

Low pressure — 60°N

High pressure — 30°N

Heated air rises and moves towards the poles.

Low pressure (ITCZ) — Equator (0°)

The air moving towards the equator forms the trade winds (see winds, below right).

Air cools and sinks.

High pressure — 30°S

Low pressure — 60°S

Warm air collides with polar air and rises.

Cold polar air

South pole (90°S)

This movement of air at the surface forms the polar winds (see right).

Air cools and sinks.

High pressure

The Coriolis effect

When air moves from high pressure to low pressure, the winds do not take the most direct possible route. They "try" to, but are deflected sideways. This is due to the rotating movement of the Earth, and is called the Coriolis effect.

The forces involved have the effect of deflecting the winds in the northern hemisphere to the right of their "intended" direction, and those in the southern hemisphere to the left. The Coriolis effect acts on the world's main air movements (see left) to determine the directions of the world's main winds.

The world's main winds

The Earth rotates in this direction.

High pressure

Polar winds

Northern hemisphere

Low pressure

Winds are deflected to the right.

High pressure

Westerlies

Low pressure

North East trade winds

Equator

Southern hemisphere

High pressure

Winds are deflected to the left.

Low pressure

South East trade winds

Westerlies — Polar winds — High pressure

At about 60°N and 60°S, cold air moving away from the poles meets the warmer air from nearer the equator. The warmer air is less dense and is forced to rise, forming areas of low pressure at the surface. This air cools and sinks again around the poles, forming a band of high pressure.

Moving air

The air around the world is on the move all the time. The main high and low pressure bands (see page 9) set up the general, long-term pattern of air movements. However, individual, small or very large high and low pressure areas are also constantly being created over different places on the surface. This causes surface movements of air (winds) between them. On any particular day, these may blow in a different, even opposing, direction to the main, general movement of the air.

Pressure differences

The creation of different highs and lows in different places is mainly due to fast high-level winds which blow around the Earth in the direction of its spin (from west to east). The strongest ones travel around at high levels roughly above 60°N and 60°S where the high level polar air is met by warmer air (see page 9). There are also weaker ones at 30°N and 30°S.

The strong winds follow wavy paths, formed because the warmer air makes more progress towards the pole over some areas than others. The winds travel fastest where the warm air pushes the greatest distance into the polar air, so they have uneven speeds, slowing down and speeding up as they travel. At their fastest they are called jet streams.

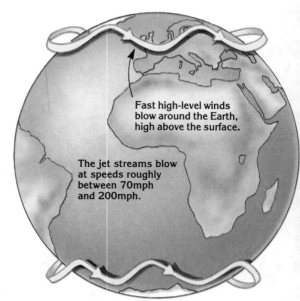

Fast high-level winds blow around the Earth, high above the surface.

The jet streams blow at speeds roughly between 70mph and 200mph.

The wavy paths (see below) and uneven speeds of the winds disrupt the air around and below them. In some areas, the air gets squashed together, so some gets pushed down, creating higher pressure at the surface. In others, the air thins out, so underlying air moves up to to fill up the space, creating lower surface pressure.

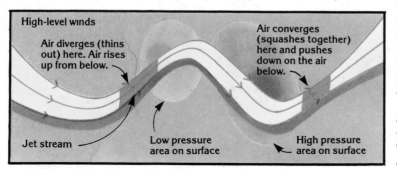

High-level winds

Air diverges (thins out) here. Air rises up from below.

Air converges (squashes together) here and pushes down on the air below.

Jet stream

Low pressure area on surface

High pressure area on surface

Because the air is disrupted, low pressure areas may form in a general high pressure band, and vice versa. The air which then moves in or away to even up the pressure may move in a different direction to the general pattern. This is because these closer pressure differences have the strongest influence.

All these air movements have a "knock-on" effect. Air becomes disrupted elsewhere, and this leads to the irregular day-to-day pattern of air movements around the globe.

Moving areas of pressure

Surface winds are always blowing from the centres of high pressure areas towards the centres of low pressure ones, but, in addition, these centres themselves are also moving. Having been created over one particular place on the Earth's surface, they are moved around by the high-level winds above them.

As the centers move, they influence each other. The closer they are, the greater this influence. If the pressure difference between a high pressure center and its surroundings is not that great, the air moving out of the high does not move very fast. So high pressure areas, with no other influences, have slow surface winds.

High pressure center at surface moves slowly, steered by high-level winds.

The center moves even more slowly than the air moving out.

The surface winds blow slowly towards surrounding lower pressure areas.

The winds feel relatively light.

Temperature and humidity

A mass of air may be warmer or colder, drier or more humid (contain more water vapor) than the air in the area it moves into. If so, it will bring a change of weather with it. Its characteristics depend on where it has come from and the type of surface it has travelled over, but also on its speed. Slow-moving air has more time to be affected by the surfaces it passes over.

Air temperature is influenced by surface temperatures. At places such as the poles and the equator, these are obviously very different, but they may also differ in areas which are quite close. One reason for this may be the different types of land which the Sun's rays fall on (see page 7), another that the areas are land and sea. At different times (in a daily cycle or a longer seasonal one), the sea may be warmer than the land, or vice versa.

Land heats up quickly, because just the surface is heated.

Sun heats land only to a shallow depth.

This means it cools down quickly as well.

Sea heats up more slowly, because it is heated to a greater depth.

Sun heats surface water.

The waves travel in a circular pattern, moving the heated water away from the surface.

Lower layers of the water are heated.

Because of this, it stores heat for longer and cools down more slowly.

The humidity of a mass of air is greater if it is travelling over the sea, as water evaporates from the sea into the air. Air which has travelled far over land tends to contain little water vapor.

If a high pressure center is close to a low pressure center, though, the pressure difference between the two areas is more acute, and the air moves faster. The larger the pressure difference, the faster the air will move, so the stronger the surface winds.

The strength of surface winds depends on the difference in pressure between two areas, and the distance between them.

High pressure area

Low pressure area

The closer two areas of different pressures are, the faster the winds will blow between them.

Strong winds mean a large pressure difference. The air moves to even it out.

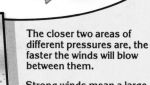

Classifying air masses

Air masses are classified according to the area they originally came from, called their source.

Air masses which form over seas and oceans are called maritime (m) air masses.

A tropical maritime (mT) air mass develops over warm seas. It is warm and moist.

A polar maritime (mP) air mass forms over the sea near the poles. It is cold and moist.

Continental (c) air masses form over land.

A tropical continental (cT) air mass develops over hot, dry land. It is warm and dry.

Polar continental (cP) air masses develop over land near the poles. They are cold and dry.

Clouds

Clouds are made up of millions of tiny droplets of water or ice crystals, formed when air is cooled. Clouds are formed in several ways and are named according to their shape, height and size. They help to forecast the type of weather which may follow. They are often associated with precipitation (rain, snow, sleet or hail), but not all clouds lead to this kind of weather.

Water vapor

Water is found in the air as an invisible gas called water vapor. This is formed when water in rivers, lakes, seas and oceans is heated. The heat makes the water evaporate (turn into vapor), and it rises into the air. The humidity of the air is the amount of water vapor it contains.

The humidity of the air varies from place to place and with temperature. When air can hold no more water vapor it is said to be saturated.

The very hot air in tropical areas (see pages 32-33) often holds a large amount of water vapor.

The air here is said to be very humid or "sticky."

How clouds are formed

Air contains millions of microscopic particles of dust. When moist air rises, expands and cools, any water vapor it contains condenses (turns back into a liquid) onto the surface of the particles. This forms minute water droplets which group together to make clouds. The temperature at which this happens is called the dew point. If the cloud temperature falls below freezing, the water droplets freeze to form ice crystals.

There are several reasons why air rises and clouds are formed.

Air may be forced to rise as it reaches high land.

Warm air cools as it is forced to rise over the higher land.

High land, e.g. a mountain range

Hill clouds form as the water vapor in the air condenses.

Air may rise by convection, when solar radiation heats the Earth's surface.

The air just above the surface is heated, becomes less dense and rises.

The warm air cools and any water vapor it contains condenses to form clouds. These are convective clouds.

Air may also rise when two air masses collide.

Warm air

Cold air

The warmer air rises above the cooler air.

Clouds called frontal clouds (see page 17) are formed.

Making a "cloud"

This experiment shows how clouds are formed as warm air is cooled. You will need a large glass jar, a small metal baking tray and some ice.

What to do
1. Pour 1 in of hot water into the jar.

2. Place some ice cubes in the baking tray and put the tray on top of the jar.

3. As the air inside the jar rises and is cooled by the ice, the water vapor it contains condenses into droplets.

Do not use boiling water as this may crack the glass.

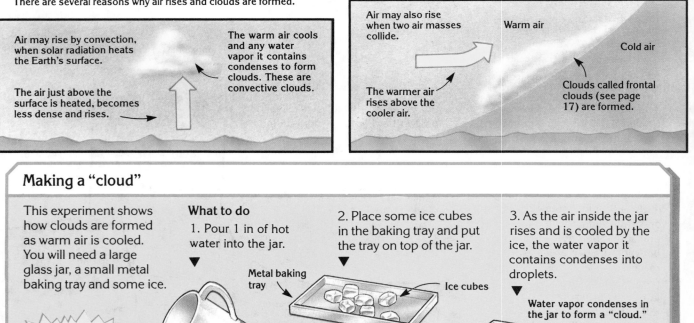

Metal baking tray

Ice cubes

Water vapor condenses in the jar to form a "cloud."

Large glass jar

Jar

The main cloud types

The main types of cloud are recognized by their shape and height. There are three main cloud types called cirrus, cumulus and stratus. There are many combinations of these clouds and different types may exist in the sky at the same time.

Cirrus clouds are high level clouds, usually found above 20,000ft. They are made up of ice crystals and have a feathery, wispy appearance.

Cumulus clouds are found at different heights. They are individual, rounded clouds with fairly flat bases. They are often seen on dry, sunny days.

Stratus clouds form a layer or sheet across the sky. They are found at low levels, below 1,650ft and often produce light rain and drizzle.

Many different cloud patterns are formed from combinations of the main cloud types. Their names refer to the types of clouds or the height at which they are found. For instance, the word 'alto' in a cloud type indicates that the clouds are middle level clouds, found between 6,500ft and 20,000ft. Stratus means layered, and nimbus indicates rain or snow is falling from the cloud.

Cumulonimbus clouds are like massive cumulus clouds. They have flat tops and may extend to great heights. They are associated with heavy rain and thunder (see page 18).

Cirrus clouds

Cirrocumulus are a combination of cirrus and cumulus clouds. They are individual clouds of ice which are sometimes arranged in rows.

Cirrostratus clouds are cirrus clouds which form a thin, almost transparent, layer over the whole sky. They often bring rain.

Altostratus clouds normally form a grey sheet of cloud across the sky. Sunlight can usually be seen filtering through this.

Altocumulus are small grey or white cumulus clouds of roughly the same size, often lying in rows and sometimes joined together.

Cumulus clouds

Nimbostratus clouds are a thick layer of grey clouds with an uneven base, which blot out the Sun completely.

Stratocumulus clouds form a sheet of rounded cumulus clouds which are almost joined together.

Stratus clouds

Measuring cloud cover

The number of clouds covering the sky is measured in oktas. The number of oktas indicates how much of the sky is covered by clouds. Oktas are measured on a scale of 0 to 8. (8 oktas means that the sky is completely covered). For example, a weather forecaster may describe the sky as having four oktas of cloud, which means that half the sky is obscured by clouds.

A sky with 3 oktas of cumulus cloud.

Aircraft trails are artificial cirrus clouds made up of ice crystals.

Aircraft trails

High-flying aircraft sometimes leave a white trail behind them when the air is very cold. The aircraft's exhaust system sends out a mixture of hot gases, containing large amounts of water vapor. The water vapor cools, condenses and freezes in the cold air, forming thin "cloud" trails. These are called contrails.

Water in the air

Water is found in the air as water vapor or as water droplets and ice crystals in clouds (see page 12), depending on the temperature of the air. The temperature of the air also determines the type of precipitation (rain, snow, sleet or hail) which may fall from the clouds.

Rain and snow

The temperature of the air in clouds determines the way that rain and snow are formed. In areas such as tropical areas, where the cloud temperature is mainly above the freezing point of 32°F, rain is formed by a process called coalescence. The clouds are made up of millions of minute droplets of water and as these droplets collide, they join together, forming larger droplets.

Gradually the droplets increase in size until they are too heavy to be kept up in the cloud by air currents and fall as raindrops.

Microscopic droplets in clouds collide.

Bigger droplets are formed as they join together, or coalesce.

Ice crystals and supercooled water droplets

The droplets freeze onto ice crystals.

The ice crystals collide and join together to form snowflakes.

Scientists think that the shape of snowflakes depends on the height and temperature at which they are formed.

In cooler areas, clouds may stretch up into air which is below freezing. These clouds are a mixture of water droplets, lower down, and ice crystals and special supercooled water droplets higher up. These droplets exist as water even though the temperature is below freezing.

As well as coalescence at the bottom, a process called accretion happens higher up in these clouds. The ice crystals attract the supercooled droplets, which freeze onto them. As the crystals grow and stick to others, snowflakes form. When they become too heavy to be held up, they fall.

In areas where the air temperature near the ground remains below freezing, snow falls, but if the temperature is above freezing, the flakes melt and fall as rain. Sleet is a mixture of snowflakes and raindrops.

Needles

Star

Plates

Hail

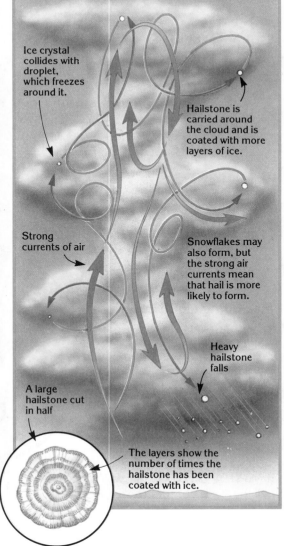

Hail forms in cumulonimbus clouds (see page 13), which have strong upward and downward currents of air moving within them. The temperature at the top of these clouds is well below freezing. As ice crystals rush around the cloud, they collide with supercooled water droplets and are rapidly coated with layers of ice.

More ice layers are added as the hailstones are swept up and down and tossed about in the cloud. They eventually fall when they are too heavy to be held up by the air currents within the cloud.

Ice crystal collides with droplet, which freezes around it.

Hailstone is carried around the cloud and is coated with more layers of ice.

Strong currents of air

Snowflakes may also form, but the strong air currents mean that hail is more likely to form.

Heavy hailstone falls

A large hailstone cut in half

The layers show the number of times the hailstone has been coated with ice.

Mist and fog

Mist and fog are "surface clouds," made up of minute droplets of water. Like clouds, they are formed when water vapor in the air condenses as it cools below its dew point. Clouds form when air is cooled as it rises, whereas fog forms when a deep layer of air is cooled by the underlying surface. Sea fog is formed when warm, moist air is cooled over a cold sea (see page 22).

The difference between mist and fog is determined by the density of the "cloud". This affects the distance which can be seen ahead, or the visibility. Fog is more dense, resulting in poorer visibility than in mist (see page 27).

The surface is cooler than the air.

Water vapor condenses.

Fog forms above the surface.

Measuring rainfall

The amount of rain or snow which falls can be measured on a rain gauge. To make a rain gauge you will need a tall plastic bottle (with a flat, clear bottom) and a ruler.

What to do

1. Use a sharp pair of scissors to carefully cut around the plastic bottle, about 4 in from the top.

No lid

Plastic bottle

Scissors

Flat, clear bottom

Top piece or funnel

2. Fit the top piece of the bottle upside-down in the bottom piece. These form the funnel and collecting jar. The funnel directs rain into the collecting jar and also forms a barrier to stop any of it evaporating.

Bottom piece or collecting jar

Rain gauge

Remember to empty the rain gauge after each measurement.

3. Sink the base of the bottle in the ground in an open area, away from trees and buildings. Use a ruler to measure the amount of rain which falls in a given time. You could make a daily record.

Ground

If you are measuring snow, you may not need the funnel. About 4½in = ½in of water.

Dew

Dew forms when air immediately in contact with a cold surface is cooled to its dew point. The water vapor condenses into dew droplets on the surface. Dew is always found when there is fog, but it may also form on a clear night when the layer of air touching the surface reaches its dew point, but the air immediately above does not.

Air directly in contact with surface cools below its dew point.

Water vapor condenses into droplets of dew on cold surfaces.

Frost

Frost occurs when the ground temperature is below freezing. The most common type is known as hoar frost. It is made up of tiny ice crystals. Some of these are frozen dew, others form when water vapor turns directly into ice as it comes into contact with a freezing surface. This happens without the water vapor passing through the stage of condensing into water droplets (dew).

On a cold winter morning, white hoar frost is often seen covering the ground.

The ground may freeze (a ground frost) without there being any white covering, if there is not enough moisture in the air.

Highs, lows and fronts

Areas of high and low pressure are constantly moving across the Earth's surface, with air moving between them (see pages 10-11). Air moving into an area brings with it the characteristics of where it has come from. Where two air masses with different characteristics meet, the air does not mix easily, but forms a boundary, called a front.

Movement of air around highs and lows

Meteorologists refer to areas of high pressure as highs or anticyclones, and areas of low pressure as lows, depressions or cyclones.

As surface winds blow into a low, and away from a high, the Coriolis effect (see page 9) makes them circulate around the pressure center.

In the northern hemisphere, air travels clockwise around a high.

It travels anticlockwise around a low.

High pressure center

Low pressure center

Air circulates in the opposite direction in the southern hemisphere.

Highs and lows on a weather map

Weather maps (see page 28) show air pressure readings at sea level. On these maps, places of equal pressure are joined by lines called isobars. Surface winds do not blow from high to low pressure directly across the isobars. Instead, they blow almost parallel to the isobars. This is because the air spirals into and out of the high and low pressure centers (see above).

The average pressure of the atmosphere has been set as 1013mb (29.91psi)*. However, areas are not marked as high or low in relation to this, but in relation to the pressure in surrounding areas. For instance, a pressure of 1008mb is marked as a low when the surrounding areas are 1032mb, but as a high when the surrounding areas have readings of 996mb.

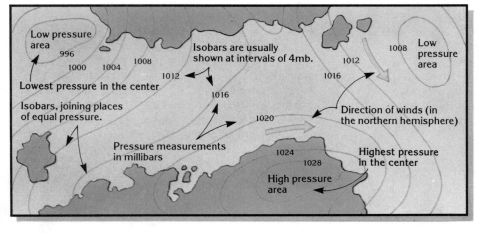

Low pressure area
996
1000   1004   1008
Lowest pressure in the center
Isobars, joining places of equal pressure.

Isobars are usually shown at intervals of 4mb.
1012
1016
Pressure measurements in millibars
1020
1024
1028
High pressure area

1008   Low pressure area
1012
1016
Direction of winds (in the northern hemisphere)
Highest pressure in the center

The Buys-Ballot law

The Buys-Ballot law states that in the northern hemisphere, if you have your back to the wind, there will be lower pressure on your left and higher on your right. In the southern hemisphere, low pressure is found on the right.

Fronts

A front is the boundary between two masses of moving air with different temperatures and humidity. The main front is called the polar front and is found around latitudes 60°N and 60°S, where cold polar air meets warmer tropical air coming from towards the equator. In some places along the polar front, the warm air mass bulges into the cold air and in others the cold air pushes out into the warm air. This is because there are uneven pressure differences along the front.

In some places the cold polar air pushes into warmer air.

60°N (latitude)

Polar front

In others, the warmer tropical air bulges into the colder air.

In general along the front, the warm air rises over the cooler air. It rises at different speeds in different places, forming areas of low pressure. The greater the temperature difference between the warm and cold air, the faster the warm air will rise. The greatest differences in temperature occur at the points where one mass of air has pushed furthest into the other. High-level winds (see page 10) may also be causing air to rise in certain places, speeding it up even more.

* mb = millibars, psi = pounds per square inch. To convert millibars to pounds per square inch, multiply by 0.02953.

Fronts and pressure

Wherever air is rising along the polar front, there is a fall in pressure. However, individual centers of low pressure are formed where the air is rising most quickly as these are the points that have the lowest pressure compared with those on either side of them. Because of these individual centers, the polar front is never seen as a continuous line, but as a series of individual fronts, occurring at the low pressure centers. These are known as frontal depressions. The surrounding warm and cold air moves towards them, because they have the lowest pressure. Winds do not blow directly into areas of low pressure, though, (see page 16), so the air circulates around them as it moves in.

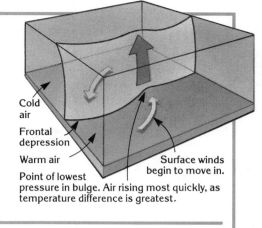

Cold air

Frontal depression

Warm air

Point of lowest pressure in bulge. Air rising most quickly, as temperature difference is greatest.

Surface winds begin to move in.

Warm and cold fronts

As the winds circulate around a frontal depression, they bring warm air into an area where there is colder air, and vice versa. This movement of air forms warm and cold fronts (as shown in the diagram below).

Where cooler air moves into a warmer area, it is known as a cold front. The cool air pushes under the warm air, forcing it to rise.

Where warm air advances into an area to replace cooler air, it is known as a warm front. The warm air rides up over the cooler air.

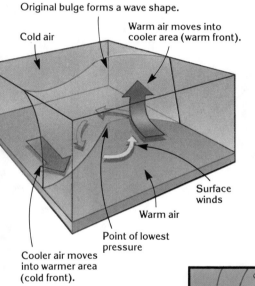

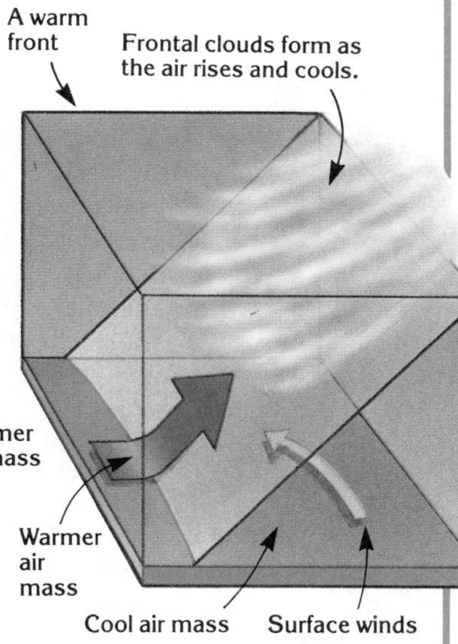

Original bulge forms a wave shape.

Cold air

Warm air moves into cooler area (warm front).

Point of lowest pressure

Warm air

Surface winds

Cooler air moves into warmer area (cold front).

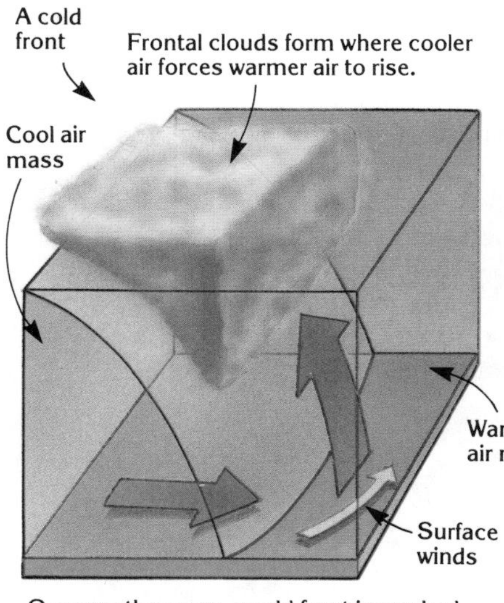

A cold front

Frontal clouds form where cooler air forces warmer air to rise.

Cool air mass

On a weather map, a cold front is marked by a line with triangles along it.

Surface winds

A warm front

Frontal clouds form as the air rises and cools.

Warmer air mass

Warmer air mass

Cool air mass

Surface winds

A warm front is marked by a line with semicircles along it.

Occluded fronts

A cold front gradually moves towards a warm front and may eventually catch it up. If it does so, it undercuts the warm air and lifts it right off the ground. The front is then described as an occluded front. This extra "push", as the cold air moves in and lifts the warm air, can produce huge clouds and very heavy rain.

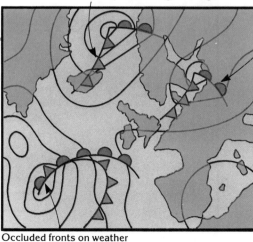

Occluded fronts on weather maps are lines with both semicircles and triangles.

Changing weather

Like all pressure areas, frontal depressions are not stationary, but are moved by high-level winds. They bring a general pattern of unsettled weather to places they pass over. Cirrus clouds are usually the first sign that a depression may be approaching, followed by a sequence of other clouds and rain. However, no two depressions produce exactly the same sequence of weather.

Thunderstorms and hurricanes

Storms are a combination of strong winds and heavy rain, snow or hail, and form in low pressure areas. Under certain conditions, minor storms can develop into thunderstorms or hurricanes, which can cause much damage to areas where they occur.

Thunderstorms

Thunderstorms form when particularly warm, moist air rises into cold air above land or sea. As the humid air rises to a great height, water vapor condenses, forming huge cumulonimbus clouds.

Water droplets and ice crystals in the clouds bump together and break up as they rub against each other in strong currents of air. This action builds up positive electrical charges at the top of the clouds and negative charges at the base.

When the charge at the base of the cloud gets to a certain strength, electrical energy is released and passes through the air to another point with the opposite charge, such as the ground. This release of energy is called the leader stroke and forms a path of charged air for the main stroke to travel along. The main stroke travels back up to the cloud and produces a flash of lightning.

Cumulonimbus cloud

At the same time as the main stroke travels up, it heats the air, causing it to expand very quickly. This expansion of air produces the sound we hear as thunder.

Leader stroke forms a charged path.

Main stroke follows path back up to cloud and produces a flash of lightning.

The air expands very quickly, producing thunder.

If the storm is directly overhead, the thunder will be heard at the same time as the lightning is seen.

If not, the lightning is seen several seconds before the thunder is heard, as the speed of light is faster than the speed of sound.

Thunder-storms die out once the charges in the clouds have evened out.

Hurricanes

In tropical areas, thunderstorms may develop into violent storms with torrential rain, and wind speeds reaching as much as 186mph.

Meteorologists call these storms tropical cyclones, but they are more commonly known as hurricanes. They are also given other names in different countries around the world, such as typhoons in S.E. Asia and willy-willies in Australia.

Hurricanes form only above tropical seas between the latitudes 5° and 20° north and south of the equator, where the sea temperature is above 80°F, and so the conditions of heat and moisture are at their most extreme.

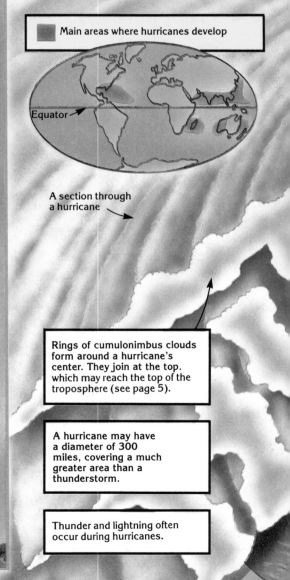

Main areas where hurricanes develop

Equator →

A section through a hurricane →

Rings of cumulonimbus clouds form around a hurricane's center. They join at the top. which may reach the top of the troposphere (see page 5).

A hurricane may have a diameter of 300 miles, covering a much greater area than a thunderstorm.

Thunder and lightning often occur during hurricanes.

The development of a hurricane

It is not fully understood why a hurricane develops, as moist air is always rising above warm seas, but it is thought that an "extra" low pressure area moving in over the sea may set them off.

As the pressure falls rapidly, strong surface winds are formed as air is sucked in towards the center of the low. At the center the air speeds up and spirals upwards. Vast quantities of water vapor in the rising air condense to form massive cumulonimbus clouds. As the water vapor condenses, enormous amounts of heat are given out which makes the air rise even faster, and in turn increases the speed of the surface winds moving in.

Naming hurricanes

Lists of alternate male and female names are drawn up each year. As soon as a storm becomes hurricane strength with wind speeds over 74mph, it is given the next name on the list.

Hurricane Gilbert in 1988 caused severe damage to islands in the Caribbean.

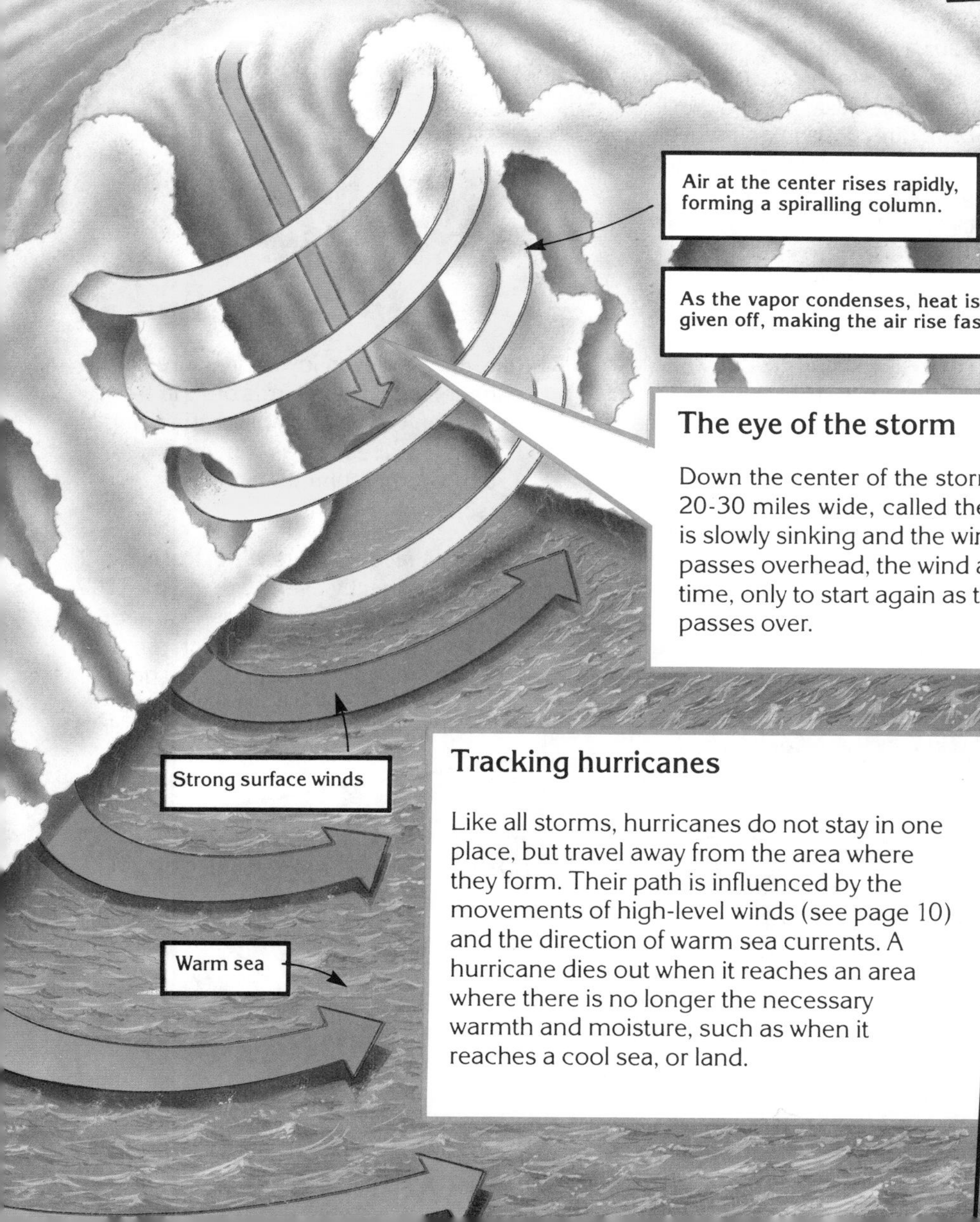

Air at the center rises rapidly, forming a spiralling column.

As the vapor condenses, heat is given off, making the air rise faster.

The eye of the storm

Down the center of the storm there is a column of air 20-30 miles wide, called the eye. The air here is slowly sinking and the winds are light. As the eye passes overhead, the wind and the rain stop for a short time, only to start again as the other side of the hurricane passes over.

Strong surface winds

Warm sea

Tracking hurricanes

Like all storms, hurricanes do not stay in one place, but travel away from the area where they form. Their path is influenced by the movements of high-level winds (see page 10) and the direction of warm sea currents. A hurricane dies out when it reaches an area where there is no longer the necessary warmth and moisture, such as when it reaches a cool sea, or land.

Satellite images are used to detect where a storm may develop into a hurricane.

Meteorologists try to predict the path which a hurricane may take, and issue warnings to people who are at risk from the storm.

A satellite image of a hurricane

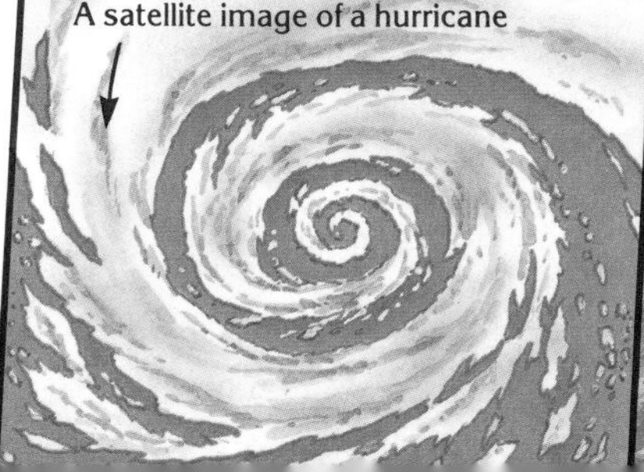

19

Extreme weather conditions

Extreme weather conditions, such as floods or droughts, sometimes interrupt the usual pattern of weather in some areas. In other places, extreme conditions are experienced each year as part of the seasonal pattern.

Droughts

A drought occurs when there is less than ⅟₁₀₀in of rain, or other type of precipitation, over a period of at least fifteen days. Droughts may occur because of a high blocking the passage of rain-bearing lows across an area (see page 21). They also occur when areas of land are cleared of vegetation in areas which are already very dry (see pictures, right).

Water vapor is given off by plants.

Moist air rises and cools, and clouds form, which may give rain.

Where there are few plants to feed many animals, they are all eaten, leaving the ground bare. This is called overgrazing.

There are no plants to give off water vapor, so no clouds form as the rising air is dry.

Flooding

Flooding may occur for several reasons, for instance, if large amounts of rain fall and there is too much water to drain away. Flooding also occurs when sea levels rise, when the land is swamped by waves caused by storms, or when snow on land melts as temperatures rise rapidly, causing rivers to overflow.

When more than ⅝in of rain falls in 3 hours, meteorologists describe the conditions as a "flash flood."

When a flash flood occurs, there is too much water to drain away. It flows rapidly across the surface, flooding areas in its path.

Monsoons

The term monsoon describes winds which blow, in tropical areas such as India and S.E. Asia, from roughly opposite directions in different seasons. The combination of the extremes of temperature and pressure in these areas, and the position of the land and the sea, produces extreme weather conditions.

This scene shows the extremely heavy rain which falls during the wet monsoon season.

One of the two winds is dry, while the other brings extremely heavy rain, so there is a dry monsoon, which creates a dry season, and a wet one which brings a rainy season.

For example, in India, the wet monsoon blows when the Sun lies almost directly overhead, and the equatorial band of low pressure, called the ITCZ (see page 9) is furthest north. The land is heated intensely, causing vast amounts of air to rise, forming even lower pressure on the surface. Very moist winds blow in from the Indian Ocean, to replace the rising air. Many places receive as much as 118in of rain during the rainy season.

The dry season occurs when the sun is no longer directly overhead and the ITCZ is furthest south. This low pressure zone causes winds to blow from high pressure over the land towards the ITCZ. These winds are dry as they have travelled a large distance over the land.

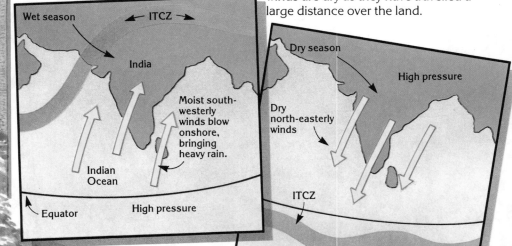

Wet season — ITCZ →

India

Moist south-westerly winds blow onshore, bringing heavy rain.

Indian Ocean

Equator   High pressure

Dry season

High pressure

Dry north-easterly winds

ITCZ

Measuring air humidity

During the wet monsoon, the humidity of the air (see page 12) is extremely high. Humidity is sometimes measured on wet and dry bulb thermometers. To make these you will need two thermometers, with scales roughly ranging from 32°F to 95°F, some cotton wool, two rubber bands and a small bowl of water.

What to do

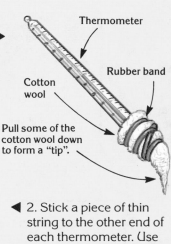

1. Wrap the bulb end of each thermometer in equal amounts of cotton wool. Secure each piece with a rubber band.

Thermometer

Cotton wool

Rubber band

Pull some of the cotton wool down to form a "tip".

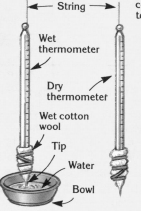

String

Wet thermometer

Dry thermometer

Wet cotton wool

Tip

Water

Bowl

2. Stick a piece of thin string to the other end of each thermometer. Use drawing pins to hang the thermometers outside in the shade. Put a bowl of water below one of the thermometers so that its tip is in the water.

3. After 30 minutes, read each thermometer. Work out the difference between the two temperatures. Use the chart to calculate the humidity of the air.

Heat is given off as water evaporates from the cotton wool, so the temperature shown on the wet thermometer will be lower than that on the dry one. If the air contains large amounts of water vapor, less water evaporates, so the temperature difference between the thermometers will be smaller, and the humidity measurement higher.

Humidity is measured as a percentage. 100% humidity is very humid and the air feels sticky.

Temperature on the dry thermometer ▼	Difference between wet and dry bulb thermometers ▼									
	2°F	3°F	5°F	7°F	9°F	11°F	13°F	14°F	16°F	18°F
50-57°F	85	75	60	50	40	30	15	5	0	0
59-66°F	90	80	65	60	50	40	30	20	10	5
68-77°F	90	80	70	65	55	45	40	30	25	20

◄ Humidity (%)

Blocking highs

Areas around 60° north and south of the equator usually experience changeable weather as areas of high and low pressure are moved across them by the high-level winds (see page 10). The wavy pattern of these winds, and the position of the waves, changes frequently, bringing highs and lows which change the weather.

High-level winds

Jet streams

Low pressure area

High pressure area

The jet streams form areas of high and low pressure at the surface and move them along, so changing the weather.

Occasionally, the movement of the low pressure areas is "blocked" by an area of high pressure which remains in one place for a long period of time and prevents any change in the weather for several days or weeks. These areas of high pressure are known as blocking highs.

If the waves in the high-level winds become very large and stay in the same position, a high may become stationary.

This blocking high may remain in one place for a prolonged period.

The weather in the area of the blocking high remains very settled for a long period.

It diverts the flow of the high-level winds, and the lows are steered around it.

Other areas experience unsettled weather because of these diverted lows.

Blocking highs can persist for several days or even weeks. They may produce prolonged cold weather, with ice and snow in winter, or very hot, dry weather in summer, which may lead to a drought.

Local weather

Coastal and mountain areas often experience local variations in winds, temperature and rainfall, which seem to have no relation to the overall weather pattern of the larger area surrounding them. Cities also frequently have different types of weather from their surroundings (see page 34).

Land and sea breezes

Coastal areas often experience land and sea breezes, which form a local circulation of air affecting areas up to 20 miles inland. The breezes may blow in a different direction from the wind blowing across the rest of the country that day.

Land and sea surfaces heat up and cool down at different rates (see page 11). Sea breezes are formed on days of high pressure when the land heats up quickly. Air rises from the land forming a local area of relatively low pressure. This air spreads out as it meets high pressure air which is sinking. At the surface, air moves in from the sea to replace this rising air. This movement of air at the surface forms sea breezes.

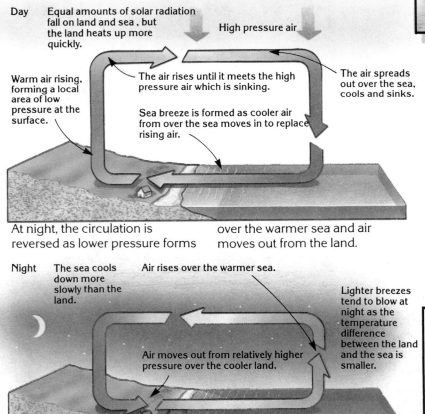

Day   Equal amounts of solar radiation fall on land and sea , but the land heats up more quickly.

High pressure air

Warm air rising, forming a local area of low pressure at the surface.

The air rises until it meets the high pressure air which is sinking.

The air spreads out over the sea, cools and sinks.

Sea breeze is formed as cooler air from over the sea moves in to replace rising air.

At night, the circulation is reversed as lower pressure forms over the warmer sea and air moves out from the land.

Night   The sea cools down more slowly than the land.

Air rises over the warmer sea.

Lighter breezes tend to blow at night as the temperature difference between the land and the sea is smaller.

Air moves out from relatively higher pressure over the cooler land.

Land and sea breezes do not form every day. For instance, on cloudy days, land and sea surfaces receive little solar radiation. This means that the temperature difference between the two surfaces is too small to start the circulation of air.

Coastal fog

Fog may be found at the coast, when there is sunshine only a short distance inland. Sea fog is formed when winds, blowing towards the coast from a warm source region, pass over the cold surface of the sea. The warm air is cooled below its dew point, forming fog (see page 15).

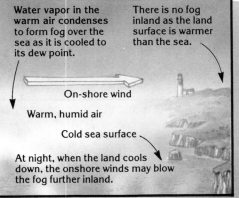

Water vapor in the warm air condenses to form fog over the sea as it is cooled to its dew point.

There is no fog inland as the land surface is warmer than the sea.

On-shore wind

Warm, humid air

Cold sea surface

At night, when the land cools down, the onshore winds may blow the fog further inland.

Ocean currents

Water travels around the world's oceans in currents, generally following the pattern of the prevailing winds which form them (see page 9). When a wind blows steadily in one direction for a long period, the moving air drags the surface of the water along, forming a current. The winds help to keep the currents moving in a steady flow.

Ocean currents can be either warm or cold, depending on where they were formed. They change the temperature of the air above them, bringing warm or cold air to places in their path.

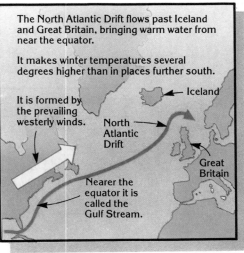

The North Atlantic Drift flows past Iceland and Great Britain, bringing warm water from near the equator.

It makes winter temperatures several degrees higher than in places further south.

It is formed by the prevailing westerly winds.

Iceland

North Atlantic Drift

Great Britain

Nearer the equator it is called the Gulf Stream.

Valley winds

Valleys often experience different weather from their surroundings. On clear, calm nights, for instance, fog often forms in valleys and light winds may blow down the mountain or hill slopes into the valley bottom. During the day, local winds may form which blow the other way, up the valley slopes.

Night   The surface cools down quickly.

The layer of air in contact with the surface is cooled most quickly. It becomes more dense and sinks, forming a light wind.

Light, cool winds blow down the mountain side and the cold air collects in the valley bottom.

Fog and frost may form if the air is cold and moist.

This mountain wind is known as a katabatic wind.

Day   Solar radiation heats the valley sides.

The layer of air in contact with the valley sides is heated most quickly.

Light winds are formed as this air rises up the valley sides.

This upslope wind is known as an anabatic wind.

Rainbows

A rainbow is an isolated optical effect caused by the Sun's rays being refracted (bent) and reflected as they pass through millions of raindrops. For a rainbow to occur there needs to be bright sunshine and rain occurring at the same time.

Light energy from the Sun is known as visible, or white, light and is actually made up of several colors.

Light rays from the Sun

Visible light enters a raindrop, is refracted and splits into separate colors.

The colored light is reflected within the raindrop.

The colors are refracted again, as they leave the raindrop.

The shape of a rainbow is due to the way that light enters the raindrops and is refracted at certain angles.

A rainbow would be seen as a complete circle if the Earth's surface was not there.

A rainbow effect

It is possible to split the Sun's visible light into its separate colors, producing a rainbow effect. For this you will need a bowl of water, a piece of white cardboard, a small mirror and a very bright, sunny day.

What to do

1. Place the bowl of water in a very sunny position. Put the mirror into the bowl and lean it against the side.

Put a stone into the water to stop the mirror from slipping.

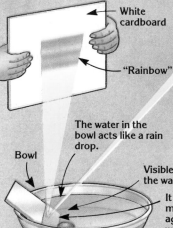

Mirror

Window

Bowl of water

White cardboard

"Rainbow"

Bowl

The water in the bowl acts like a rain drop.

2. Adjust the angle of the mirror so that a strong beam of sunshine falls on its surface. Move the cardboard around in front of the bowl, until a reflected "rainbow" appears on it.

Visible light is refracted as it enters the water.

It is then reflected by the mirror and refracted again as it leaves the water, producing a rainbow effect.

23

Monitoring the weather

In order to forecast the weather, meteorologists use information collected around the world. This information is based on observations made at the same time every day, at weather stations and elsewhere, using a variety of methods.

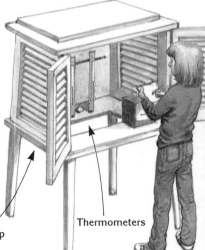

Weather stations

At weather stations, observers use a variety of instruments to monitor such things as wind speed, clouds, air temperature and pressure. They also record the general weather, such as if it is raining or foggy.

The methods and equipment used at every station are standardized, so the weather is monitored in exactly the same way.

Air temperatures are measured on the thermometers inside a Stevenson screen. The shuttered sides allow air to flow freely, but keep the thermometers out of direct sunlight.

Thermometers

Aircraft and ships

Many aircraft and ships provide weather information about areas where there are no weather stations. Like automatic weather stations on land (see below), they have equipment which records different weather conditions along their routes.

Many aircraft fly at an altitude of between 30,000-40,000ft.

They provide useful information about high-level winds.

Ships provide information about weather conditions at sea.

This information is sent via satellite to a processing station on shore.

Automatic weather stations

Automatic weather stations are positioned in areas such as mountains or polar regions, where it would be difficult to have an observer permanently monitoring the weather. Computers are programmed to take readings from the weather instruments every hour.

An automatic weather station in Antarctica

Automatic stations are unable to provide information about cloud types, current weather conditions or visibility.

Radiosondes

The temperature, humidity and pressure at different heights above the ground are recorded by instruments called radiosondes. These are carried high into the air by balloons.

The speed, direction and rate of ascent of the rising balloon indicate the strength and direction of the wind. As the balloon rises through the air, the temperature, humidity and pressure readings are taken by the radiosonde. Signals from radiosondes are transmitted to places called processing stations on the ground.

Balloon

The balloon takes about an hour to rise to 60,000ft.

It continues to rise until the pressure of the surrounding air becomes so low that the balloon bursts.

After it bursts, a small parachute opens and the radiosonde falls to the ground.

Radiosonde

Radiosondes are released from weather stations twice a day.

Many are lost, as they fall into the sea or land in remote areas. Some are returned to the weather stations by people who find them.

Weather satellites

Weather satellites provide essential information about the location and movement of weather systems, and the pattern of clouds around the Earth. Two types of weather satellite orbit the Earth.

Geostationary satellites orbit at a height of 22,400 miles above the equator.

Geostationary satellites orbit the Earth once every 24 hours, the same time the Earth takes to spin around its axis. This means that they always monitor the weather above the same place on the Earth's position.

Polar orbiting satellite

Earth's rotation

Polar orbiting satellites orbit the Earth from pole to pole at a height of 530 miles.

Polar orbiting satellites take about 100 minutes to complete one orbit, passing over both the Arctic and Antarctica. Each time they complete one orbit, the Earth has rotated by 25° longitude. This means a different strip of the Earth's surface is monitored on each orbit.

Satellite images

Weather satellites carry instruments called radiometers, which sense the intensity of reflected light or heat. This information is turned into images (pictures) at processing stations. The satellites are useful in locating and tracking the paths of weather systems, particularly over large oceans.

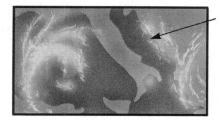

A visible satellite image

Different surfaces, such as cloud tops, land, water and ice reflect different amounts of sunlight. These different amounts show up as different shades of white or grey. These images cannot be produced at night as there is no light.

An infrared satellite image

Infrared images are produced from measurements of heat, not light. The temperatures of different surfaces are recorded to produce these images. Infrared images of the Earth can be produced during the day and at night.

Radars

Weather radars are used to show where there is rain, hail or snow and how heavily they are falling. Radar systems work by sending out waves of radiation which bounce off rain drops and are reflected back, like echoes, to a receiving dish. The information is then sent, often via a satellite, to a processing station where it is turned into an image.

Radar images are color-coded to show where the heaviest precipitation is occurring.

White lines are coastlines

The heaviest rain is coloured yellow.

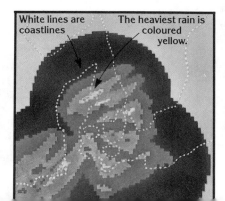

A wind vane

All weather stations have a wind vane which indicates the direction of the wind. To make a wind vane you will need some thin cardboard, adhesive book covering film, 40in of ⅛in dowel, glue, strong sticky tape, two cable clips and a pen lid.

What to do

1. Draw out the wind vane on the cardboard and cut it out. Cover one side with the film and score a line down the center.

Cardboard

Covering film (for waterproofing)

4¾in

3in

9¾in

1in

4¾in

2. Fold the vane in half. Stick the folded halves together (covered sides outwards) and cut across the narrow end to make a pointer. Use the tape to stick the pen lid to the vane.

Fold in half along the scored edge.

Pen lid

Pointer

3. Get someone to hold the dowel against a wooden post and attach it with the cable clips, so that the dowel does not turn.

Place the vane on top of the dowel. Make sure it spins freely.

Wind

Dowel

Cable clips

4. Find reference points, such as trees or walls, for north, south, east and west, using a map or compass. The wind turns the vane until the pointer is pointing in the direction the wind is blowing from.

Remember, a wind is always named by the direction it blows from.

If the pointer is pointing to the east, the wind is blowing from east to west, so an easterly wind is blowing.

Your own weather station

Professional observers at weather stations around the world (see page 24) make regular observations to record weather conditions. By making daily observations and using simple equipment, you can set up your own weather station and begin a logbook to record your local weather.

Choosing a site

It is very important that the equipment used for recording different weather conditions is not affected by its surroundings. It is best to place the equipment in a relatively open area, such as a garden, but away from trees and tall buildings.

Buildings and other obstacles can affect the speed and direction of the wind.

Obstacles cause wind eddies, where the air swirls and even changes direction.

Drips from buildings or trees will affect rainfall amounts.

Wind direction and speed

Wind direction is monitored on a wind vane (see page 25), which needs to be sited away from any obstacles. Wind speed is usually measured by an anemometer (but see below).

Anemometer

The cups rotate in the wind.

The stronger the wind, the faster they spin around.

Temperature

Temperatures which are recorded at weather stations are taken in the shade (see page 24). You can make recordings by hanging a thermometer on a fence or a wall which is in the shade.

The highest and lowest temperatures can be recorded on maximum and minimum thermometers. You can buy these at a garden center.

Minimum thermometer

Maximum thermometer

As the temperature rises or falls, the liquid in each thermometer moves an indicator. The indicator will remain at the highest (maximum thermometer) or the lowest (minimum thermometer) temperature reached.

Measuring wind speed

In order to measure wind speed at your weather station, you could make a simple wind box. You will need a shoe box, sticky tape, some thin cardboard, a knitting needle, a protractor, plastic film and a fine, permanent-ink pen.

Protractor

Pen

Scale

Plastic film

What to do

1. Using the protractor and the permanent-ink pen, mark the angles for a wind-speed scale, at 5° intervals between 0° and 90° on the plastic film.

2. Cut the ends off the shoe box and lid, and stick them together. Cut a hole in one side of the box, near to one end (see below), and stick the scale inside, so it is displayed through the hole.

Lid

Scale

Hole

Do not cut away this corner

Shoe box

Make a small, round hole here.

3. Push the knitting needle through the small, round hole (see previous picture), and wiggle it about until it rotates freely. Cut out a cardboard flap, slightly smaller than the end of the box. Stick it to the needle.

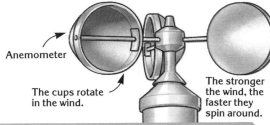

Flap

Knitting needle

4. Hold the box so the flap faces into the wind. Look at the angle of the flap and work out the wind speed from the table below.

Angle (°)	mph	Angle	mph
90	0	40	21-22
85	5-7	35	23-24
80	7.5-9	30	25-27
75	9.5-10.5	25	27-30
70	11-12.5	20	30.5-33.5
65	13-14		
60	15-15.5		
55	16-17		
50	17.5-19		
45	19-20.5		

Wind direction

Flap

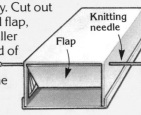

Visibility

Visibility is recorded as the distance a person can see. On a clear day, write down various landmarks you can see, such as a church or some hills. If your own weather station is in an area where the view is restricted, you could use a local open space to record the visibility. Use a map of your area (your local library should have one) to measure the distance from your recording point to each landmark.

Estimate the visibility by recording the furthest landmark you can see that day.

When visibility is less than 3,000ft, it is said to be foggy.

Visibility is poor when you can see for between 3,000ft-3 miles.

Clouds

Weather observers record the cloud types. They also record the cloud cover measured in oktas (see page 13).

Abbreviations are used to indicate each cloud type.

Cirrus – Ci	Stratus – St
Cirrocumulus – Cc	Altostratus – As
Cirrostratus – Cs	Stratocumulus – Sc
Cumulus – Cu	Nimbostratus – Ns
Altocumulus – Ac	Cumulonimbus – Cb

Visibility is said to be moderate when you can see for 3-6 miles.

Visibility is said to be good when you can see for more than 6 miles.

Pressure

Air pressure is measured on a barometer which should be placed inside a building. You can use your home-made barometer (see page 8) to record whether the pressure is rising or falling. You could also find out the exact pressure reading from your local weather center.

The barometer should be placed away from direct sunlight. It should also be placed away from sources of heat, such as radiators and fires.

In your logbook, use arrows to indicate whether the pressure is rising or falling, or remaining the same.

Humidity

The humidity of the air is measured on wet and dry bulb thermometers (see page 21), which should be placed in the shade.

Precipitation

You can measure rainfall and other types of precipitation with your rain gauge (see page 15). Make sure it sits well away from trees and buildings.

Wet and dry bulb thermometers

A weather logbook

Try to take your observations at the same time each day. Start a logbook in which you can record all your readings. Also record the general weather, such as if it is raining or sunny. You could use the weather symbols on page 28 to record your observations.

Date	Time	Pressure Rising or Falling	Wind Speed	Wind Direction	Cloud Oktas	Cloud Type	Visibility	Temp	Humidity	Precipitation	General weather
1st Jan	08.00	↓	5-7 mph	SW	8	Ns	poor	39.2F	100%	.07in	rain
2nd	08.15	→	7.5-9 mph	W	8	St	poor	42°F	95%	.2in	drizzle

Analyzing information

Weather observations, taken at weather stations all over the world (see page 24), are gathered together and distributed by special communication links to national weather centers in many countries, where all the information is analyzed and weather maps are produced.

Incoming information

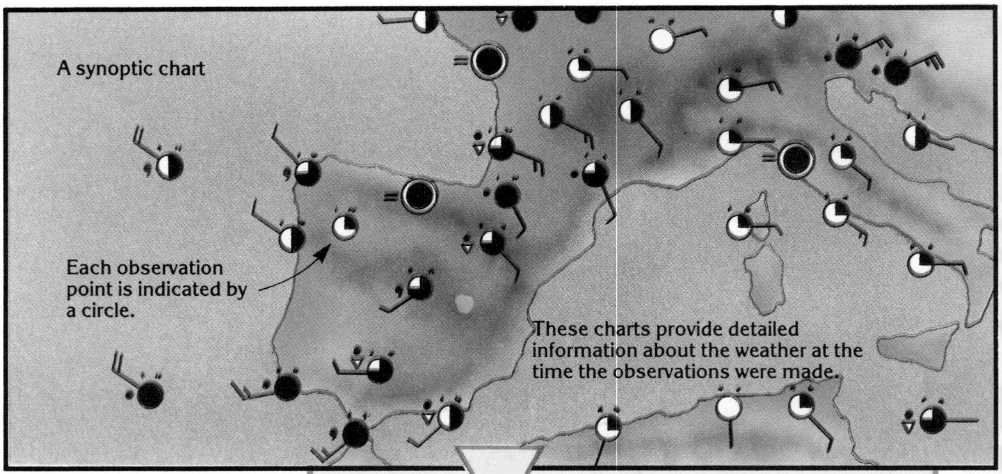

The information received at national weather centers includes observations made at manned and automatic weather stations, and on ships and aircraft, as well as information from processing stations, such as radiosonde readings, and satellite and radar images.

Some of these observations are turned into weather maps called synoptic charts, such as the one above right.
These use many different symbols to show the different readings. The key on the right shows the main symbols.

Every day, in addition to producing synoptic charts, the centers produce a computer model of the atmosphere (see page 29), based on the information they receive. After all their analyses are complete, they make the results available to those who need them.

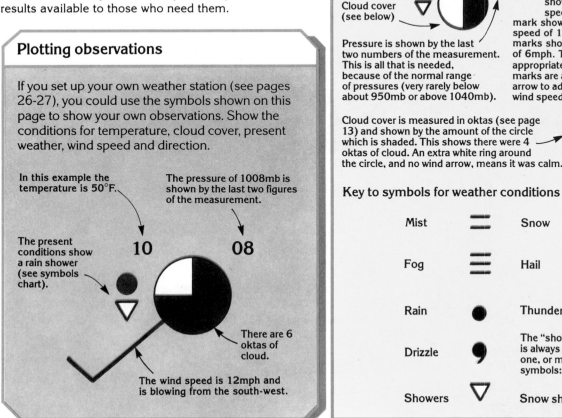

A synoptic chart

Each observation point is indicated by a circle.

These charts provide detailed information about the weather at the time the observations were made.

Key

Temperature (in °F).

Present weather conditions (see below)

Cloud cover (see below)

Wind "arrows" indicate the direction from which the wind is blowing.

A north-easterly wind

Marks on the arrow show the wind speed. Each whole mark shows a wind speed of 12mph. Half marks show a speed of 6mph. The appropriate number of marks are added to the arrow to add up to the wind speed.

Pressure is shown by the last two numbers of the measurement. This is all that is needed, because of the normal range of pressures (very rarely below about 950mb or above 1040mb).

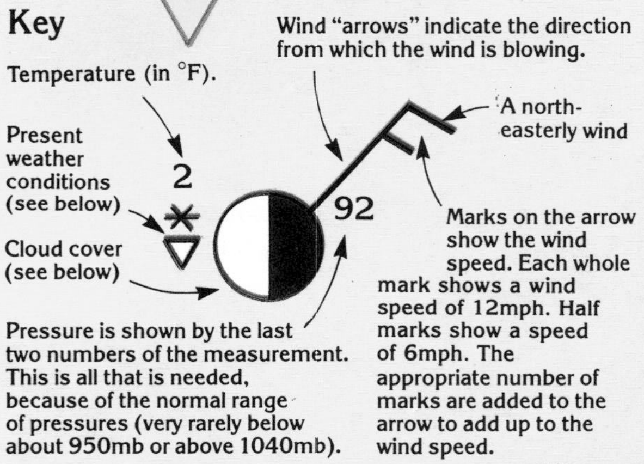

Cloud cover is measured in oktas (see page 13) and shown by the amount of the circle which is shaded. This shows there were 4 oktas of cloud. An extra white ring around the circle, and no wind arrow, means it was calm.

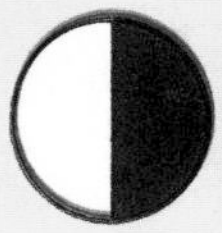

Plotting observations

If you set up your own weather station (see pages 26-27), you could use the symbols shown on this page to show your own observations. Show the conditions for temperature, cloud cover, present weather, wind speed and direction.

In this example the temperature is 50°F.

The pressure of 1008mb is shown by the last two figures of the measurement.

The present conditions show a rain shower (see symbols chart).

10   08

There are 6 oktas of cloud.

The wind speed is 12mph and is blowing from the south-west.

Key to symbols for weather conditions

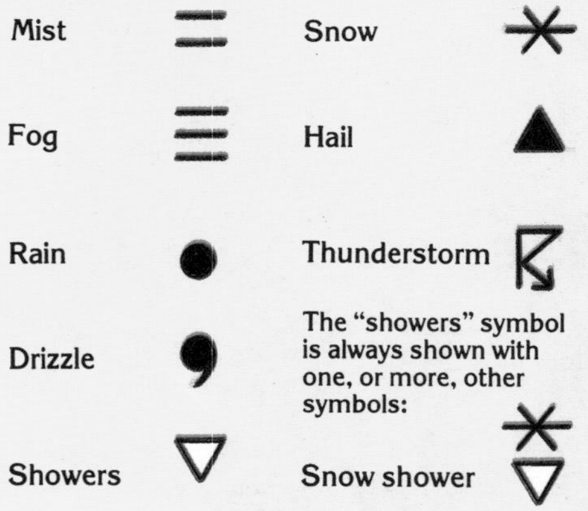

Mist	=	Snow	✳
Fog	≡	Hail	▲
Rain	●	Thunderstorm	�
Drizzle	,	The "showers" symbol is always shown with one, or more, other symbols:	✳ ▽
Showers	▽	Snow shower	

Computer models

Meteorologists use computers to predict what may happen to the weather for a period of time ahead. Using information from observations, calculations are made on computers to produce a model of the atmosphere as it was at the time when the observations were made. This model uses numbers to represent all the values for temperature, humidity, wind and pressure at different levels in the atmosphere.

Grid points

In order for the computer to predict what may happen to the atmosphere, all the different readings made at different levels have to be arranged in a regular pattern in the model. Imaginary lines of longitude and latitude divide the Earth's surface into a grid. The points where the lines meet are called grid points, and the readings are assigned to these points. In most cases, the actual observations were not made at places exactly on these grid points, but the readings are allotted to the grid point nearest to where they were made.

In areas where there is little or no information, the computer estimates conditions using readings from surrounding grid points and past information about the weather.

There are 40,000 imaginary grid points covering the Earth's surface.

The computer has readings for temperature, pressure, winds and humidity, not just for each grid point, but also for points at many levels directly above it.

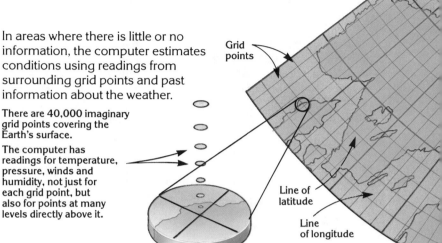

Grid points

Line of latitude

Line of longitude

Predictions

To make a prediction, the computer calculates changes that should occur to each set of grid point numbers in a short space of time ahead, usually ten minutes. This produces a new set of numbers for the computer to use. This "time-step" process is repeated many times, until the computer predicts, for instance, what the temperature and winds will be like twelve hours ahead. This whole process takes only a few minutes and then computer maps and charts are produced, based on the predictions, which weather forecasters can use.

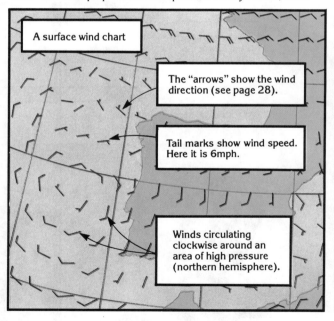

A surface wind chart

The "arrows" show the wind direction (see page 28).

Tail marks show wind speed. Here it is 6mph.

Winds circulating clockwise around an area of high pressure (northern hemisphere).

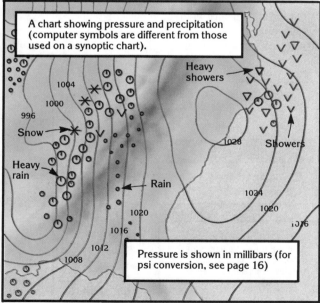

A chart showing pressure and precipitation (computer symbols are different from those used on a synoptic chart).

Heavy showers

Snow

Heavy rain

Rain

Showers

1004
1000
996
1028
1024
1020
1020
1016
1016
1012
1008

Pressure is shown in millibars (for psi conversion, see page 16)

Computer predictions about the weather twelve hours and twenty-four hours ahead are produced at national weather centres twice a day. The time-step process is usually continued to give predictions for up to a week ahead. These predictions may not be very accurate, however, because each time the time-step process is repeated, any small errors, which were present in the original grid point calculations, will reappear and become magnified. This is the reason why many long-term weather forecasts are often unreliable.

Weather forecasts

In order to predict the weather for the hours and days ahead, forecasters analyse information they receive from national weather centers (see pages 28-29). They look at the computer predictions but also use the observation maps and satellite images to make their own predictions. Forecasts reach the public via television, radio, newspapers and telephone information lines.

Weather forecasters

Weather forecasters work in many different places, such as the national weather centers themselves, or at separate city weather centers or meteorological offices at military and public airports.

They study all the information they receive and look closely for things such as fronts, highs and lows, which may bring a change to weather patterns. They also often add their knowledge of frequent local weather conditions, such as coastal fog (see page 22).

Forecasters at city weather centres have direct contact with some public services.

Severe weather conditions, such as fog, snow and ice greatly affect road transport.

When ice is expected, the relevant department can be alerted, so the roads can be sprayed with salt.

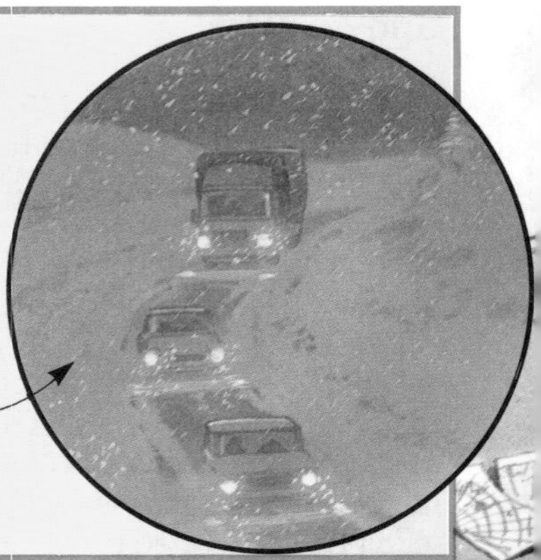

Television forecasts

Many weather forecasters on television are trained meteorologists. They make their own forecasts, using the large variety of information sent to them directly from a national weather center. Other forecasters are television presenters who read out forecasts provided by a weather center. The forecaster's predictions for the day ahead are presented as a sequence of weather maps, which have been drawn up on computers in the graphics department of the television center. These weather maps may show, for example, temperatures, winds or a summary of the expected weather conditions. The forecasters also use "movies" (individual geostationary satellite images joined together) to show the movement of weather systems.

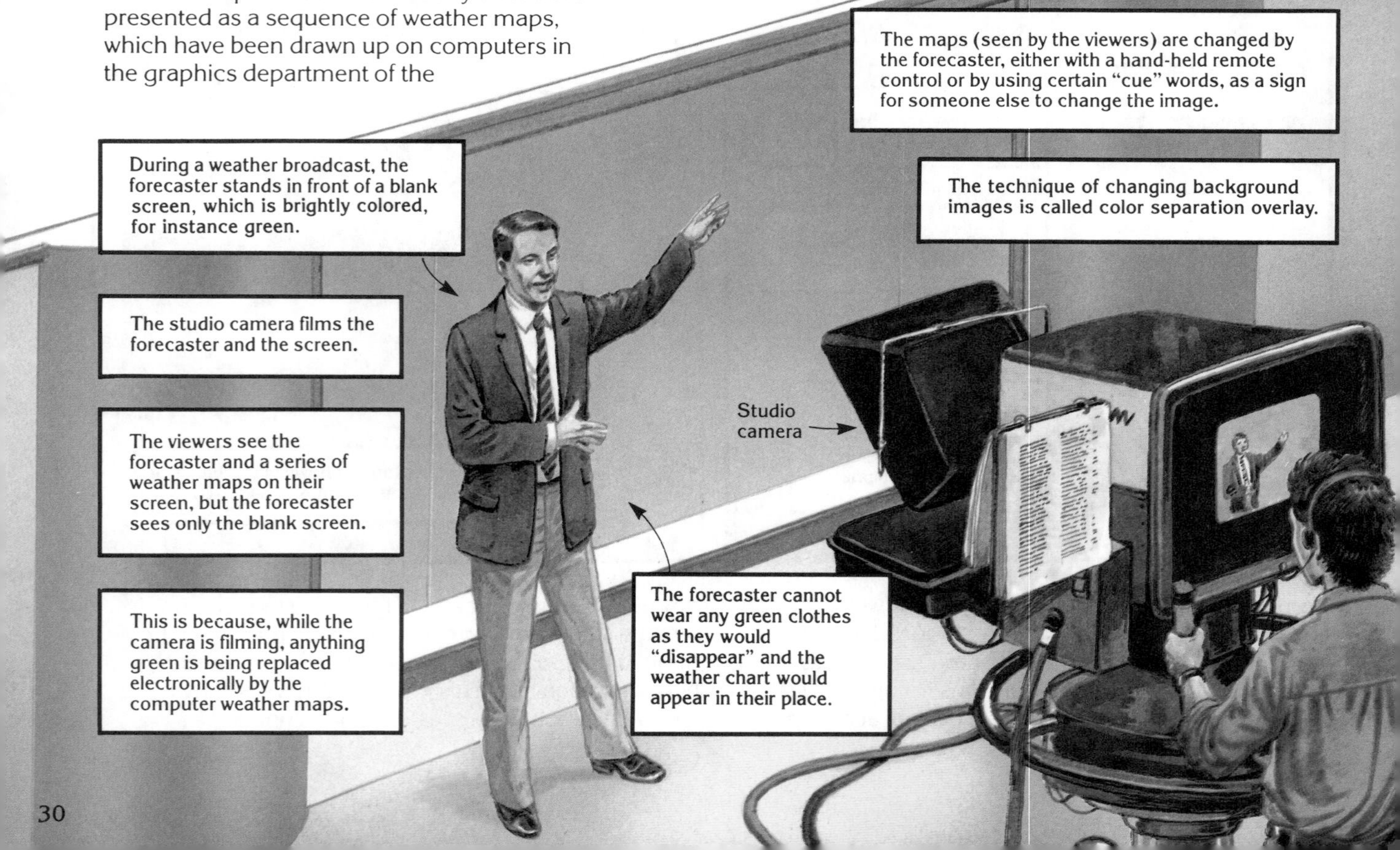

The maps (seen by the viewers) are changed by the forecaster, either with a hand-held remote control or by using certain "cue" words, as a sign for someone else to change the image.

The technique of changing background images is called color separation overlay.

During a weather broadcast, the forecaster stands in front of a blank screen, which is brightly colored, for instance green.

The studio camera films the forecaster and the screen.

The viewers see the forecaster and a series of weather maps on their screen, but the forecaster sees only the blank screen.

This is because, while the camera is filming, anything green is being replaced electronically by the computer weather maps.

Studio camera

The forecaster cannot wear any green clothes as they would "disappear" and the weather chart would appear in their place.

Radio and newspaper forecasts

Meteorologists at national and city weather centers provide radio stations and newspapers with information for their weather reports. National radio stations give a very generalized forecast for the whole country. Local radio stations, like local television stations, provide a more detailed forecast for their particular area. Newspaper forecasts are not as up-to-date, as the information they use has been issued at midday on the day before it appears in the newspaper.

Stormy conditions, such as high seas, create dangers for people who work at sea, so detailed advance warnings are needed. Some radio stations broadcast a specialized shipping forecast. These give warnings of severe weather conditions along with the expected wind speed and direction.

Up-to-date weather forecasts are particularly important for people who work at sea, e.g. on ships and oil rigs.

A meteorologist analyzing satellite images, charts and maps

A television monitor next to the camera shows the forecaster what the viewers are seeing, and helps him point to the correct places on the blank screen.

Who uses forecasts?

Weather forecasts are used by many specialized services, as well as being of interest to the public. Forecasts of approaching bad weather, such as storms or poor visibility, are of particular importance to aircraft, airports, shipping and fishing boats. Destinations can be changed, or routes diverted, to avoid bad weather conditions.

Specialized farming forecasts are broadcast on some television and radio stations. Farmers need to know if there is likely to be a severe frost, or if it is going to rain when they sow, harvest or spray their crops.

Farmers need to know when to spray crops with fertilizers or pesticides. If it rains within a few hours of the field being sprayed, the chemicals will be washed away and have no effect on the crops.

How accurate are forecasts?

Weather forecasters try to be as accurate as possible, but their predictions are not always correct. You could compare the forecasts given for your area, over a period of days. Make a chart for recording the accuracy of forecasts from newspaper, television, radio and telephone.

Record your own weather observations (see pages 26-27) and compare your records with the forecasts.

A forecast is fairly accurate if the wind speed is within 5mph and the temperature is within 4°F of your readings.

Mark your chart with ticks or crosses depending on whether you think the forecast is accurate.

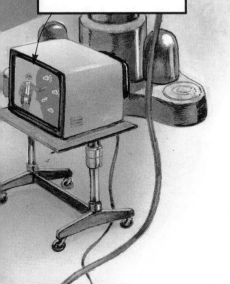

		Actual measurements	Newspaper		T.V.		Radio		Telephone	
Sunday	Temp.	62.6°F	60.8°F	✓	60.8°F	✓	62.6°F	✓	57.2°F	✗
	Wind	7.4 mph	8.7 mph	✓	9.3 mph	✓	7.5 mph	✓	9.3 mph	✓
	General weather	rain	showers	✓	showers	✓	clear	✗	rain	✓
Monday	Temp.									
	Wind									
	General weather									

Worldwide climate

The climate of a particular area is the average pattern of weather which it experiences, measured over a long period. There are many different types of climate in different areas around the world, and these have a great effect on the vegetation and animals found there.

Climates around the world

World climates are classified into different types, mainly by latitude and temperature. Within each main type, variations may occur. For instance, coastal areas have maritime or mediterranean climates, whereas places in the centre of large continents have continental climates. When naming a climate, these variations are combined with the main types. For instance, a coastal area in the tropics has a tropical maritime climate.

The world's main climate types

☐ Arctic or polar. Very cold and dry, strong winds. Summer temperatures may be 50°F near coasts, but much lower inland. Some areas also classified as deserts.

☐ Cold. Short summer, warmest month between 50°F and 59°F. Cold winter, averaging -4°F to -22°F. Low rainfall, usually in summer.

▨ Mountain. Temperature and rainfall depend on the latitude and change according to height.

☐ Cool temperate. Between one and five months of temperatures below 43°F. Rainfall throughout year. Warm summers but cold winters, often below freezing.

▨ Warm temperate. Mild, wet winters with temperatures between 39°F and 50°F. Hot summers, 68°F to 81°F, with little rain.

☐ Desert. Annual rainfall below 10in. In hot deserts, temperatures during the daytime may exceed 125°F.

▨ Monsoon. A hot, wet season and a cool dry season, caused by winds which change with the season (see page 20).

☐ Tropical. Temperatures high all year, between 75°F and 81°F. High humidity. Heavy rain throughout year near equator (called equatorial climate), over 80in per year. Other regions have most rain in one season.

Equator

Water loss from plants

Plants take in water through their roots and use it to make their food, but some water evaporates through tiny pores in their leaves.

To show that plants from different climates lose water vapor at different rates you need two 2-quart clear plastic bottles, a house plant, a cactus, two plastic bags, wire bag ties and plates, and some petroleum jelly.

What to do

House plant, e.g. geranium

Cactus

Wire tie

Plastic bag

Pot

1. Give each plant approx. 3 fl.oz of water. Place each pot in a bag and fasten around the base of each plant with the wire ties. Place each plant on a plate.

2. Using a pair of scissors, carefully cut the base off each bottle.

Base

Scissors

Plastic bottle

3. Place a bottle over each plant. Smear a thick layer of jelly around the base of each bottle.

Bottles (keep lids on)

Petroleum jelly

The jelly stops moisture from escaping.

Place each plate in a light, sunny position.

4. After three days, you should see water droplets on the inside of the bottles. These have condensed from water vapor given off by the plants.

Water droplets

More vapor should have been given off by the house plant.

The cactus comes from a desert where water is scarce. It loses very little water through its leaves (spines).

Climate and living things

Plants and animals are found in all areas of the world, each type adapted to the climate of its area. The fewest species are found where conditions are harshest, such as at the poles, and the greatest number in areas with much kinder climates. The most variety occurs in the warm, wet tropical areas.

Tropical rain forests

Rain forests are found in tropical areas near the equator, where there is over 80in of rain a year. Temperatures are high, as, because of their position, these areas receive most solar energy (see page 6). Over half the Earth's species of plants and animals live in rain forests.

In tropical rain forests, it rains in short, heavy showers nearly every day. The warm, humid conditions provide the ideal living conditions for plants and animals.

Scarlet macaw

Surviving in deserts

In hot deserts, daytime temperatures are very high as there is hardly any cloud cover to protect the surface from the Sun's rays. It cools down quickly at night as heat radiates into space. There is little rain each year but fog and dew may form when the air cools at night. The few plants and animals which live in these regions have developed ways of surviving the intense heat and scarcity of water.

Ocelots hunt for their prey in forest trees and on the ground.

Toucan

Some animals, such as the head-standing beetle, rely on fog or dew for water. The fog condenses on to its body, and it tilts forwards, so the droplets run into its mouth.

Many desert animals, including the head-standing beetle, escape the fierce heat by burrowing under the surface.

Many desert plants can store water in special cells when it rains. This means they can survive through the long, dry periods.

Leaf succulents have leaves which swell up to hold water.

Squirrel monkey

Plants known as bromeliads grow on the trunks and branches of trees.

Red-eyed tree frogs live in the rainwater which collects in their leaves.

Cacti store water in their stems. They also have spines instead of leaves. These have a much smaller surface area, so lose less water through evaporation.

Surviving freezing temperatures

There are relatively few species of animals or plants living near the poles, where the temperature is nearly always below freezing.

In Antarctica, temperatures may fall below -40°F.

Penguins are protected from the freezing temperatures by very dense feathers and a thick layer of fat under their skin.

Emerald tree boa

Giant armadillo

People and climate

People live in all the different climates of the world, ranging from the polar areas to the equator. In order to live a comfortable life, particularly where the climate is harsh, they have designed their houses, clothes and lifestyles to fit the conditions of their particular climate.

Building design

Most buildings are designed to make living in a particular climate as comfortable as possible. In temperate climates, with seasonal variations in temperature, many buildings have thick walls which trap the heat which builds up inside them. Many of these buildings are heated artificially in winter by fires and central heating. Windows are designed to let in maximum amounts of sunlight in winter and let out excess heat which builds up during the day in summer.

In temperate areas, houses are designed to keep heat in during the winter.

Large windows are often positioned on the sunniest side of the house to allow in as much sunlight as possible in the winter. These can be opened in summer to allow heat to escape.

Thick curtains help to keep in the heat in winter.

In hot climates, houses are designed for coolness. Most have few walls or partitions, to allow the maximum amount of air to circulate. Some buildings have window shutters, which are closed during the hottest part of the day, to keep the hot air out, and opened in the early morning and evening to allow cool air to circulate around the building.

In tropical areas, many houses have few inside walls. This allows air to circulate freely inside the building.

In areas of heavy rain, roofs are often built with a steep pitch (angle) to allow the water to drain off easily.

Houses are built on stilts in tropical areas to avoid being flooded during heavy rain.

City climates

Cities tend to have a different climate to their surrounding area because of their high concentration of buildings. They tend to be warmer at night, and may also get more rain in summer. The amount of pollution in the air also tends to be higher in cities (see page 40).

Tall buildings act as barriers to the wind. This either forces the wind upwards, or funnels it along the streets between buildings.

If the air rising over the city is exceptionally warm and humid, it may cool to form clouds, which may give short bursts of rain.

Building materials, such as bricks, stone and concrete, absorb a great deal of heat during the day.

At night, this heat is given off slowly, forming a "heat island", which makes a city up to 9°F warmer than its surroundings.

Reflecting the Sun's heat

Different surfaces absorb and reflect different amounts of solar energy (see page 7). Light-colored and shiny surfaces reflect the Sun's rays and so reduce the amount of heat that materials absorb.

In countries with a hot, sunny climate, buildings are often painted white, to reflect heat away. People also often wear light-colored clothes to reduce the amount of heat their bodies receive.

In hot climates, buildings are white-washed to reflect the heat and help keep them cool.

People who live in extremely hot climates, such as deserts, wear long robes to protect them from the Sun and from wind-blown sand.

Just as few walls help air to move around inside a house, flowing robes help to circulate air around a body, keeping it cool.

The body and temperature

The human body reacts to different temperatures with various mechanisms which help it adjust its own temperature. Normally a person's body gives off heat, as it is warmer than the surrounding air. This heat is lost from the blood in blood vessels just under the surface of the skin.

When a person gets very hot, extra body heat is given off by sweating. As water evaporates from the skin, the body temperature is lowered. More heat is also lost from the skin's blood vessels, as these widen to allow more blood through.

When it is very cold, the blood vessels constrict, or become narrower, letting less blood through, so less heat is lost from the body. In extremely cold conditions, the supply of blood to some parts of the body, usually fingers and toes, may stop completely.

The blood travels into the surface blood vessels from the main arteries, and out of them via the veins.

Artery   Vein

The blood is pumped around all the blood vessels by the heart, and picks up heat as it travels.

If fingers and toes receive no blood, they receive no heat. The skin "dies". This is known as frostbite.

Making a radiometer

A radiometer is an instrument which uses reflection and absorption to measure solar energy. To make a simple radiometer, you need a black pen, a chewing gum wrapper, a jam jar, a pencil, some foil, strong glue, thread and a used matchstick.

What to do

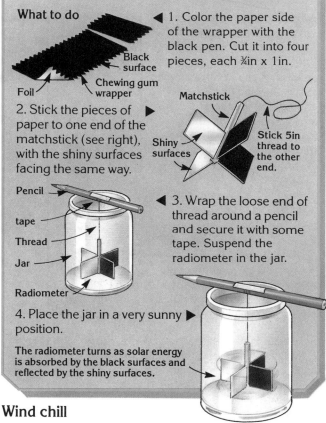

Black surface

Chewing gum wrapper

Foil

1. Color the paper side of the wrapper with the black pen. Cut it into four pieces, each ¾in x 1in.

Matchstick

2. Stick the pieces of paper to one end of the matchstick (see right), with the shiny surfaces facing the same way.

Shiny surfaces

Stick 5in thread to the other end.

Pencil

tape

Thread

Jar

Radiometer

3. Wrap the loose end of thread around a pencil and secure it with some tape. Suspend the radiometer in the jar.

4. Place the jar in a very sunny position.

The radiometer turns as solar energy is absorbed by the black surfaces and reflected by the shiny surfaces.

Wind chill

The wind can make the air temperature feel colder than it actually is. This is called the wind chill factor. Normally, a thin layer of warm air surrounds your body, but if the wind is strong, this warm air is blown away, making you feel colder.

If the air temperature is 32°F and a gentle breeze is blowing, the wind chill factor makes it feel like 27°F. If the wind speed increases to a strong breeze, the temperature feels like 14°F.

Scientists who work at the poles wear several layers of clothes to help insulate their body against freezing temperatures and the wind.

The clothes trap air which is warmed by the scientists' body heat, keeping them warm.

Changing climates

The Earth was formed about 4,600 million years ago, but the climate has not always been as it is today. At certain times, covering periods of thousands of years, it was much warmer than it is now. At other times, it was a lot colder, with much of the land covered in ice.

The first atmosphere

When the Earth was first formed, the atmosphere as we know it did not exist. The Earth's surface was a mass of liquid rocks which cooled to form a solid crust. As it cooled, the primitive atmosphere was formed from steam and poisonous gases, given off by erupting volcanoes.

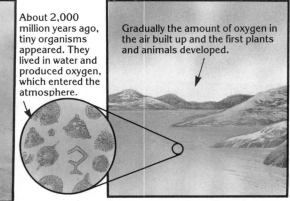

About 3,500 million years ago there was no oxygen in the air.

There was also no ozone layer yet, to protect the Earth from the Sun's high-energy rays.

About 2,000 million years ago, tiny organisms appeared. They lived in water and produced oxygen, which entered the atmosphere.

Gradually the amount of oxygen in the air built up and the first plants and animals developed.

Ice ages

In the past, the Earth has gone through periods of time, called ice ages, when the climate was much colder and ice sheets covered huge areas of the surface. At the moment, ice sheets are found at the poles, but at times, ice has covered much larger areas.

Present-day ice sheet

Scientists think that ice ages have occurred about every 100,000 years and that they last for about 75,000 years. At the moment, the climate is between ice ages. This is called an interglacial climate.

Ice sheets are still found in the Arctic and Antarctic.

There are several theories which try to explain why ice ages occur. In the past, some scientists believed that the climate became colder because at certain times the amount of energy given off by the Sun decreased.

Ice ages have also been explained by a change in the Earth's angle of tilt on its axis and a change in the path of the Earth's orbit around the Sun.

The ice which forms the ice sheets has built up over thousands of years.

Climate change due to moving continents

The climate of each continent may have also changed because its position gradually changes. This is because the Earth's crust is made up of several pieces, called plates, which move very slowly, carrying the continents with them. Millions of years ago, many countries may have had a different climate because they were not found in the same latitude as they are today.

200 million years ago scientists believe there was one "supercontinent" called Pangea.

Antarctica was in much warmer latitudes.

India was much further south.

Gradually the continents moved to their present-day positions.

The Earth's present orbit around the Sun is almost a circle.

Over thousands of years the shape of the orbit may have gradually changed to an oval and back to a circle. This would have changed the amount of solar energy the Earth received. When the orbit changed to an oval, an ice age may have occurred as the Earth became cooler.

Volcanic eruptions

Scientists believe that erupting volcanoes may affect world climates. When a volcano erupts, fine volcanic dust may be thrown high into the atmosphere. The dust acts as a screen, reflecting more solar radiation back into space and preventing it from reaching the Earth.

It is thought that when the Earth was first formed, thousands of volcanoes covered the surface. Poisonous gases and dust, thrown out as the volcanoes erupted, greatly affected the climate.

Large volcanic eruptions still occur today, but they are very rare and their effect on the climate is short-term. Records show that the weather may be affected for two or three years following a huge eruption.

When Tambora in Indonesia erupted in 1815, volcanic dust was flung high into the atmosphere.

Dust from Tambora was spread around the world by high-level winds. Temperatures fell as the amount of solar radiation reaching the Earth decreased.

Climate change and the extinction of the dinosaurs

About 65 million years ago more than half the species of plant and animal life, including the dinosaurs, became extinct. Scientists believe that a sudden change in climate could have caused the mass extinction.

Dinosaurs existed on Earth for over 150 million years. During that time, the climate was believed to be warm and humid.

Some scientists believe that many species became extinct due to a massive volcanic eruption which blocked out the sunlight. This caused green plants to die, as they need sunlight to produce their food. In turn this meant many plant-eating animals died out.

Other scientists believe that a massive asteroid (immense rock in space), with a diameter of about 9 miles, may have hit the Earth. The impact sent huge amounts of dust into the atmosphere, blocking out solar radiation.

Geological evidence

Most rocks are formed in layers, and by studying these layers, geologists (scientists who study rocks and their formation) are able to work out what the climate may have been like when each layer was formed.

Geologists use other methods to work out the age of the layers. By studying the minerals which make up a rock, they can date when rocks were formed. Once they have dated the layers, they can work out when climatic changes took place.

Rocks formed in warm climates contain a greater variety of fossils, compared with those formed in cooler times.

Rocks which lay at the surface during ice ages show evidence of being eroded, or worn away, by glaciers, or masses of moving ice.

Counting tree rings

Scientists work out climatic changes by studying the layers in rocks. In a similar way, by looking at the growth rings in the trunk of the tree which has fallen or died, it is possible to work out what the weather may have been like when it grew.

Each year the water-carrying tubes, or xylem, add new layers of cells in the centre of the tree's trunk, pushing the trunk outwards. In a year which has a warm, wet growing season more layers of cells will be added, producing a wide growth ring. In a season which has been dry or cold, the growth ring will be narrow.

You can work out the age of the tree by counting the rings.

A narrow growth ring shows that the growing season was cold and dry.

A wider growth ring indicates that the weather in that year was probably warm and wet.

This tree was 16 years old.

Present-day climate changes

At present, many scientists believe that world climates may be changing. They think this is due to the weather being affected by rising temperatures, caused by a build-up of certain gases in the atmosphere.

The greenhouse effect

The greenhouse effect is the term used to describe how the Earth is kept warm by heat trapped by gases in the lower atmosphere. It has been occurring for millions of years. Without the greenhouse effect, it is thought that the average temperature on the Earth's surface would be 5°F.

The gases, such as carbon dioxide and water vapor, are known as greenhouse gases, as they act like greenhouse glass. They let the Sun's high-energy radiation pass down through them to heat the Earth's surface, but absorb the lower energy radiation which the Earth sends back up. They then send out even lower energy in all directions. Some of this reaches the Earth, which receives extra heating.

High-energy radiation travels in through the glass of a greenhouse.

This is absorbed by the objects inside, which heat up. They send out lower energy radiation, which the glass absorbs.

The glass sends some radiation back, giving the objects extra heat.

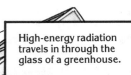

In a similar way, the Earth's surface receives extra heating as greenhouse gases absorb and send out lower energy radiation.

Global warming

At present, average temperatures around the world are gradually rising. This is known as global warming. There could be a number of reasons for this, but many scientists link it with a known increase in greenhouse gases. They believe this has led to more heat being trapped, and that it is mainly due to man's activities.

The amount of carbon dioxide in the air has increased by 25% in the last hundred years.

Power stations and factories which burn fossil fuels (coal, oil and gas), give off carbon dioxide as they produce power.

Carbon dioxide is also given off as forests are cleared and burned, to make way for farmland and building.

The scientists believe that if the amount of greenhouse gases continues to rise at its present rate, average temperatures will increase by between 3°F and 7°F in the next fifty years. Many people agree with them, and are trying to reduce the amount of greenhouse gases released into the atmosphere.

Other greenhouse gases

Carbon dioxide and water vapour are the main greenhouse gases, but other gases, such as chlorofluorocarbons (CFC's), nitrous oxides and methane, also absorb out-going radiation. The amount of these gases is also increasing.

CFC's are given off by aerosol sprays and refrigerators.

CFC's are also thought to destroy ozone in the stratosphere (see page 40).

The effects of global warming

If world temperatures continued to rise, it would greatly affect world climates and the lives of people and wildlife.

There would be more rain in tropical areas, as the extra heat would increase the amount of water vapour in the air. Areas which receive little rain would receive even less, and turn into deserts, so people and animals would have to move away.

Sea temperatures would rise and this might lead to flooding in low-lying areas and an increase in the number of severe storms.

Nitrous oxides come from car exhaust fumes and from fertilizers used on fields.

Methane is given off from rotting vegetation and swamps. Growing rice in water-filled paddy fields to feed millions of people has meant creating man-made swamps which give off more methane.

Many animals kept for food give off methane as a waste gas.

The amount of trash people produce has increased. Methane is given off from rotting trash in refuse dumps.

If temperatures rose, many animals would not be able to adapt to the climate changes.

Many plants would die for lack of water, and animals would have to migrate, or move to other areas, in search of food and water.

If many plants die due to rising world temperatures, many species of animals could die out.

Rising sea levels

If world temperatures increase, sea levels may rise, for two main reasons. Firstly, when water is heated it becomes less dense and expands. If the sea temperature rose, its level would rise as the water expanded.

Secondly, higher temperatures could melt some of the ice which permanently covers some land, such as Antarctica and certain mountains. The water would eventually flow into the sea, making it rise. The melting of ice floating in the sea, however, would not add to rising sea levels.

The Arctic ice-cap is a huge, floating sheet of ice.

Like Antarctica, the Arctic is surrounded by floating icebergs.

Even if all the ice in the Arctic melted, it would not cause a rise in sea levels. This is because when ice melts, the water which is left occupies less space than it did as ice.

Melting ice

The Arctic ice-cap floats on the sea. It would have little effect on the sea level if it melted. To carry out an experiment to show this, you need some ice cubes, a large glass bowl and a ruler.

What to do

1. Half-fill the bowl with water. Add ten ice cubes, and measure the water height.

Make sure all the ice cubes are floating in the water.

2. Wait for the ice cubes to melt.

3. Once the ice cubes have melted, measure the height of the water again.

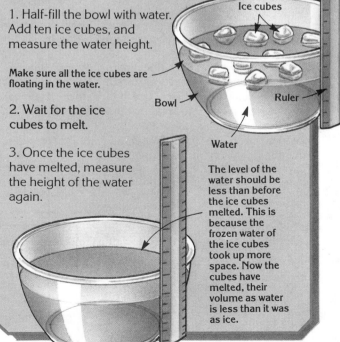

Ice cubes

Bowl

Ruler

Water

The level of the water should be less than before the ice cubes melted. This is because the frozen water of the ice cubes took up more space. Now the cubes have melted, their volume as water is less than it was as ice.

Pollution in the atmosphere

Air pollution is caused by any undesirable substance which enters the atmosphere and upsets the natural balance. These substances may be gases, liquids or solids, and are known as pollutants. Most pollutants are given off into the air as a result of human activities.

The ozone layer

Ozone is a gas, found throughout the Earth's atmosphere, but concentrated particularly in a layer in the stratosphere (see page 5). This layer is important because the molecules of gas stop harmful high-energy solar radiation from reaching the Earth's surface. Scientists have discovered that the ozone layer is getting thinner.

They think that substances in man-made gases called CFC's (see page 38) are rising into the stratosphere and breaking down the ozone molecules and that, if this continues, more and more harmful radiation will reach the Earth's surface. Exposure to harmful high-energy radiation can cause some forms of skin cancer.

Above Antarctica, scientists have discovered a "hole" where the ozone layer is thin.

They monitor the amount of ozone in the atmosphere using instruments attached to balloons.

Temperature inversions

In certain unusual conditions, a layer of warm air may trap colder air beneath it for several days at a time. This is called a temperature inversion.

When a temperature inversion occurs above a city, it greatly affects the build-up of pollutants, such as smog (smoke and fog). Normally, pollutants are dispersed, or scattered, through the atmosphere by moving air. The inversion prevents the air from rising, and traps the polluted air at a low level.

Warm air

Cooler air

Smog is formed as water condenses onto tiny particles, given off as fossil fuels are burned.

The air cannot rise as it is trapped beneath the warm air, so the pollution builds up.

Smog is not as common as it used to be. This is due to fewer buildings being heated by coal fires, and fewer power stations in cities.

Smog affects people with asthma and other breathing problems.

Surface ozone and photochemical smog

Some ozone, known as surface ozone, is found at ground level. It is a form of pollution and can cause health problems. It is formed by the chemical reaction of different pollutants with strong sunlight. The main pollutants in this case are nitrogen oxides and hydrocarbons from exhaust fumes.

When a large quantity of surface ozone builds up, it is known as photochemical smog. This is virtually invisible at street level, but can be seen as a brown haze hanging above a city.

Photochemical smog is an increasing problem in large cities in the summer.

Pollutant gases build up in the air at low levels and react with sunlight to produce surface ozone (photochemical smog). It causes people to suffer from eye irritations and sore throats.

Lead pollution

Lead is another air pollutant. It enters the air as particles from exhaust fumes, and is found much more in cities than in rural areas. Scientists believe that if people are exposed to large amounts of lead, it will build up in their blood and cause brain damage.

Lead-free petrol is now widely used to cut down on the amount of lead which pollutes the air.

Acid rain

Rainwater normally contains tiny amounts of acid, but this causes little damage. When mixed with some pollutants, though, it becomes much more acidic, and produces harmful rain known as acid rain.

Many animals cannot survive the higher acid levels, for example in lakes and rivers. Trees and other plants suffer as the acid makes them less resistant to frost and to attack by insects and diseases.

Acid rain also eats into and dissolves the surfaces it lands on, such as rocks. Harmful minerals are washed out of some rocks, and these do further damage to animals and plants (see picture, below).

Pollutants such as sulphur dioxide and nitrous oxide make rainwater more acidic. They enter the air in exhaust fumes, and when fossil fuels are burned.

Acid rain clouds may be blown for long distances before the rain falls.

Acid rain falls.

Harmful minerals, such as aluminium, are washed into rivers and lakes from dissolved rocks.

High concentrations of some minerals can affect plants and animals.

Aluminium reduces the amount of oxygen which fish can absorb through their gills, eventually causing them to die.

Aluminium from dissolved rocks affects plant roots, stopping them absorbing other, essential minerals.

The pollutants mix with water **vapor and a chemical reaction** occurs, producing droplets of sulphuric and nitric acid.

In some of the worst-affected areas, there are no fish left in rivers and whole forests have been killed.

Acid rain indicator

Most rainwater is slightly acidic. To make an indicator to see how acidic your rain is, compared with other substances, you need some red cabbage, white vinegar, baking soda, a jug and some jars.

What to do

1. Collect some rainwater in a jar. Chop up 3 large cabbage leaves. Put them into a saucepan with 1 pint of tap water. Boil them gently for ten minutes.

2. Let the mixture cool, then pour the liquid through a sieve into the jug.

3. Test your indicator liquid by pouring ½in depth into two jars. Add a few drops of vinegar to one and ½ tsp of baking soda to the other.

4. In the same way, use your indicator to test some rainwater to see how acidic it is.

The pinker the indicator, the more acidic the substance being added to it.

Red cabbage leaves

Sieve

Teaspoon

Vinegar

Baking soda

Blue/purple liquid (indicator liquid)

Baking soda is an alkali and should turn the indicator green.

Vinegar is an acid and should turn it pink.

The jar with vinegar added can be used as a comparison.

Rainwater

41

Predicting future weather

With the current concern about global warming (see page 38), meteorologists are trying to predict what effect rising temperatures may have on weather and climates around the world in the future. They use computer models to work out future climates, in a similar way to forecasting daily weather (see page 29).

General circulation models

Scientists use computer models, called general circulation models, or GCM's, to predict future weather patterns. Their computers contain vast amounts of information, about the atmosphere, such as its composition of gases, average surface and upper air temperatures and humidity, as well as information about oceans.

By changing particular pieces of information, for instance by adding more greenhouse gases, scientists can create new models which show what effect global warming may have on weather in the future.

GCM's have predicted that in continental regions, such as in North America, rainfall may increase in winter and temperatures may rise by 4.7°F in the next fifty years.

There could also be a 3-5°F temperature rise in summer, with less rain.

This change in climate could greatly affect the amount of wheat which is grown in the vast areas of North America, known as the prairies.

Uneven temperature increases

Using general circulation models, scientists have predicted that there may be an average temperature rise of 2.7°F by the year 2050. They think that temperatures will rise unevenly, though, with the greatest rise at the poles. This will have an increase of up to 7°F, compared to 1.8°F in tropical areas.

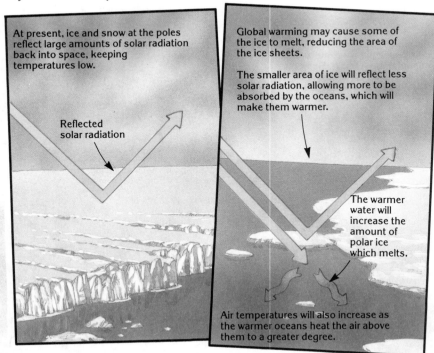

At present, ice and snow at the poles reflect large amounts of solar radiation back into space, keeping temperatures low.

Reflected solar radiation

Global warming may cause some of the ice to melt, reducing the area of the ice sheets.

The smaller area of ice will reflect less solar radiation, allowing more to be absorbed by the oceans, which will make them warmer.

The warmer water will increase the amount of polar ice which melts.

Air temperatures will also increase as the warmer oceans heat the air above them to a greater degree.

Predicted temperature increases around the world

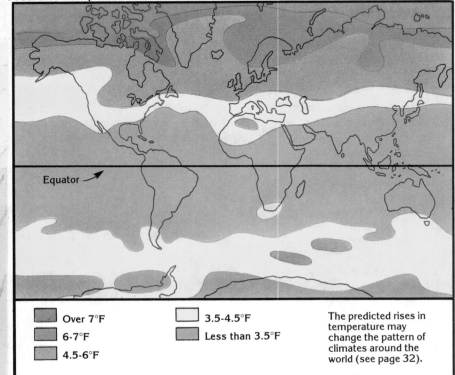

Equator

Over 7°F	3.5-4.5°F	
6-7°F	Less than 3.5°F	
4.5-6°F		

The predicted rises in temperature may change the pattern of climates around the world (see page 32).

Changing cloud cover

Some scientists believe that in a warmer world there would be more clouds, as greater amounts of water would evaporate from seas. This could lead to many areas having more rain than they do now. Also, some types of cloud reflect solar radiation, while others absorb radiation from the Earth's surface. Depending on the type and amount of "new" cloud, the rate at which global warming occurs could be affected.

If the number of clouds increases, the rate of global warming may be reduced, or even halted, but it may also be increased. Whether temperatures increase or decrease may depend on the type of clouds which are formed.

More storms?

Some scientists believe that extreme weather conditions, such as storms, hurricanes and floods could become more frequent in a warmer world, particularly in tropical areas. Even though the temperature increase in tropical areas may be small, the warmer temperatures could lead to more hurricanes, as there would be a greater area of sea with temperatures above 80°F (see page 18).

Hurricane winds produce massive waves, called storm surges.

As a hurricane approaches land, waves crash on to land causing damage and severe flooding.

If there are more hurricanes, low-lying areas already at risk from rising sea levels may also suffer from more storm surges.

In 1991, the coast of Bangladesh was hit by a storm surge which killed thousands of people.

Other scientists believe that storms could become less frequent, particularly in temperate areas. Areas of low pressure, which lead to storms, develop because of the large temperature difference between polar and tropical air (see page 16). Due to the predicted uneven increase in world temperatures, this difference would become smaller, so, according to these scientists, fewer severe storms would occur.

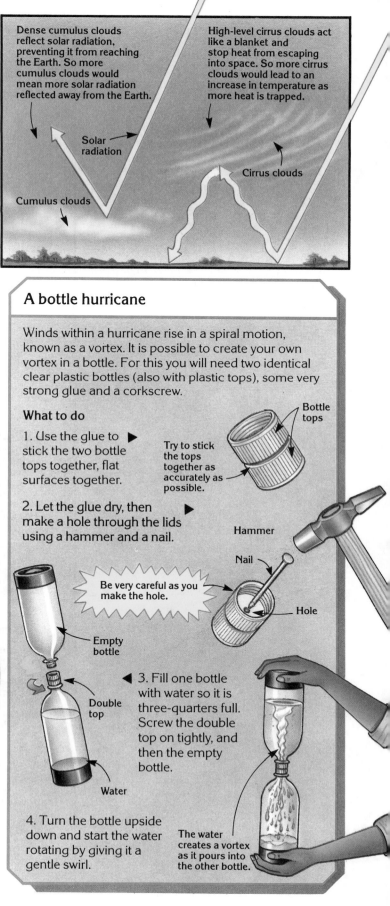

Dense cumulus clouds reflect solar radiation, preventing it from reaching the Earth. So more cumulus clouds would mean more solar radiation reflected away from the Earth.

High-level cirrus clouds act like a blanket and stop heat from escaping into space. So more cirrus clouds would lead to an increase in temperature as more heat is trapped.

Solar radiation

Cirrus clouds

Cumulus clouds

A bottle hurricane

Winds within a hurricane rise in a spiral motion, known as a vortex. It is possible to create your own vortex in a bottle. For this you will need two identical clear plastic bottles (also with plastic tops), some very strong glue and a corkscrew.

What to do

1. Use the glue to stick the two bottle tops together, flat surfaces together.

Try to stick the tops together as accurately as possible.

Bottle tops

2. Let the glue dry, then make a hole through the lids using a hammer and a nail.

Hammer

Nail

Be very careful as you make the hole.

Hole

Empty bottle

3. Fill one bottle with water so it is three-quarters full. Screw the double top on tightly, and then the empty bottle.

Double top

Water

4. Turn the bottle upside down and start the water rotating by giving it a gentle swirl.

The water creates a vortex as it pours into the other bottle.

43

Record weather extremes

Record-breaking weather and climate conditions have been monitored by meteorologists all around the world.

The rainiest climate

The wettest place in the world, with the highest number of rainy days each year, is Mt. Wai-'ale-'ale on the island of Kauai in Hawaii. It rains on as many as 350 days each year.

The Hawaiian islands lie in the Pacific Ocean. The south-east trade winds blow here, all year. These winds are warm and moist.

The winds cool as they are forced to rise over Mt. Wai-'ale-'ale.

Dense clouds form and heavy rain falls on the windward side of the mountain.

The average annual rainfall here is 451in.

By contrast, places on the leeward side, or sheltered side, of the mountains receive as little as 10in each year. This is because the winds are warmed as they descend, and contain less water vapor.

Places on the sheltered side are said to be in a rain shadow.

Longest drought

The driest place in the world, which has also experienced the longest drought, is Calama in the Atacama Desert in Chile. It is said that up until 1971 there had been no rain there for 400 years.

The Atacama Desert receives very little rain because it lies in the rain shadow of the Andes mountain range.

Equator (0°)

Atacama Desert

The south-east trade winds lose their moisture as they rise over the Andes.

Andes Mountains

As well as being in a rain shadow, the Atacama Desert is dry because it lies in the high pressure band around latitudes 30°S (see page 9), so the air is sinking.

Any warm thermals (see page 7) cannot rise very far due to the sinking air, so no clouds are formed.

30°S

Hottest climate

Dallol in Ethopia, on the eastern edge of the Sahara Desert, has an average annual temperature of 93.9°F, making it the hottest place in the world.

Clouds greatly affect the amount of solar radiation which reaches the Earth's surface (see page 43).

Few clouds are found above the Sahara Desert, which lies in the band of permanent high pressure at roughly 30°N (see page 8).

Here, air from tropical regions further south sinks towards the Earth's surface.

The air becomes warmer as it sinks, so any water vapor it contains does not condense to form clouds.

The hot surface greatly heats the air above it.

The highest air temperature ever recorded was at Al 'Aziziyah in Libya, which is also at the edge of the Sahara Desert. The temperature reached 136.4°F in the shade (meteorologists always measure temperatures in the shade – see page 24).

Coldest climate

The coldest climate in the world is in Antarctica. Scientists at the Plateau research station in Antarctica have kept records which show the average annual temperature to be –69.8°F.

The lowest air temperature was also recorded in Antarctica, at the Russian research station in Vostok. The temperature fell to –128.6°F.

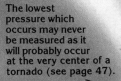

Snow reflects over 90% of solar radiation back into the atmosphere.

The surface receives very little heating, so the air above remains very cold.

The lowest number of hours of sunshine is also found at the south pole. The Sun does not rise for 182 days each year, due to the tilt of the Earth (see page 6).

Air pressure and wind speed

The highest recorded air pressure occurred in Agata, in northern Siberia. The pressure of the air at sea level reached 1083.8mb (32 psi).

The lowest air pressure, which measured 870mb (25.69 psi), was recorded in the centre of Typhoon (hurricane) Tip which occurred above the Pacific Ocean in 1979. A U.S. Air Force aircraft flew into the eye of the hurricane (see page 19) to measure the pressure.

The highest recorded surface wind speed of 280mph was caused by a tornado in Texas, USA.

The lowest pressure which occurs may never be measured as it will probably occur at the very center of a tornado (see page 47).

It is unlikely that a barometer could be positioned at exactly the right place to measure the pressure.

It is also unlikely that any instrument would survive the incredibly strong winds caused by tornados.

Observing wind speed

The speed of the wind is usually measured on an anemometer, but it can be estimated using a scale called the Beaufort scale. The scale is based on the effect of the wind at different speeds.

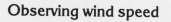

Force → ← Description   Speed →

0. Calm. Smoke rises vertically.

0mph

1. Light wind. Wind direction shown by smoke.

1-3mph

2. Light breeze. Wind felt on face, leaves rustle.

4-7mph

3. Gentle breeze. Leaves and twigs constantly move, flags begin to flutter.

8-12mph

4. Moderate breeze. Dust and paper blown about, small branches on trees move.

13-18mph

5. Fresh breeze. Small trees sway, small waves on lakes.

19-24mph

6. Strong breeze. Large branches on trees move, difficult to use an umbrella.

25-31mph

7. Near gale force. Whole trees sway, difficult to walk against the wind.

32-38mph

8. Gale. Twigs broken off trees, very difficult to walk.

39-46mph

9. Severe gale. Chimney pots and roof tiles break off.

47-54mph

10. Storm. Seldom occurs away from coasts, trees uprooted, buildings damaged.

55-63mph

11. Violent storm. Very rarely occurs, widespread damage.

64-73mph

12. Hurricane. Total devastation.

74+mph

Glossary

Acid rain. Rain which contains water droplets that have absorbed pollutants from the atmosphere and become unusually acidic. The term is also used to describe dry pollutants which fall on to surfaces from the air.

Anemometer. An instrument used for measuring the speed of the wind. ▼

Anticyclone. An area of relatively high air pressure, also known as a high.

Atmospheric pressure (air pressure). The weight of air pushing down on a planet's surface.

Barometer. An instrument which measures air pressure.

Beaufort scale. A scale used for measuring the strength of the wind, based on observations.

Blocking high. A high pressure area which remains stationary and diverts the normal path of lows across an area of the Earth's surface.

Climate. The weather conditions experienced in an area over a long period.

Cold front. The boundary between a mass of cold air and a mass of warmer air where the cold air is moving in to replace the warmer air.

Computer model. A representation of the atmosphere created by a computer, used by meteorologists to produce a weather forecast.

Condensation. A process by which a gas or vapor changes into a liquid.

Convection. The upward movement of air which has been heated by the land or sea surface below.

Coriolis effect. The effect caused by the Earth's rotation which appears to deflect air as it moves between two places.

Cyclone. An area of low pressure. It may also be called a low or a depression.

Dew point. The temperature at which water vapor condenses to form water.

Evaporation. A process by which a liquid changes into a gas or vapor.

Front. The boundary that separates two masses of air of different temperature.

Geostationary satellite. A weather satellite which stays above the same place on the Earth's surface.

Global warming. An overall increase in world temperatures which may be caused by additional heat being trapped by greenhouse gases, such as carbon dioxide and CFC's.

Greenhouse effect. The heating effect caused by gases in the atmosphere trapping heat (radiation) from the Earth's surface.

Humidity. The amount of water vapor in the air.

Ice ages. Periods of time when ice covered large areas of the Earth's surface.

Intertropical Convergence Zone (ITCZ). A band of low pressure, formed around the equator, where warm air rises and is replaced by air moving in from the northern and southern hemispheres. ▼

Isobar. A line on a weather map joining places which have equal atmospheric, or air, pressure.

Jet stream. The strongest currents of the high-level winds which circle the Earth between 6 miles and 10 miles above the surface.

Meteorologist. A scientist who studies all the elements of the atmosphere which combine to form the weather.

Monsoon. A wind which blows from different directions at different times of the year, creating a wet, or rainy season, and a dry season.

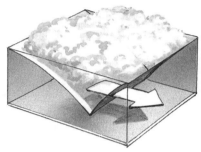

Occluded front. A front which occurs where a cold front moves in and undercuts a warm front, lifting the warm air away from the surface.

Ozone layer. A layer of ozone gas, found in the upper atmosphere, which absorbs harmful solar radiation.

Polar front. The boundary where cool air moving in from polar regions meets warm tropical air.

Polar orbiting satellite. A weather satellite which travels over both the north and south poles each time it completes one orbit of the Earth.

Precipitation. Any form of moisture, such as rain, snow, sleet or hail, that falls to the ground from a cloud.

Prevailing wind. The most common wind which tends to blow in any given location.

Radiosonde. An instrument, attached to a balloon, which monitors pressure, temperature and humidity at different heights above the Earth's surface.

Smog. Fog mixed with air pollutants, such as smoke, which cause the fog to become more dense.

Solar radiation. Heat and light energy from the Sun.

Synoptic chart. A chart which shows various elements of the weather, such as temperature and pressure, monitored in different places at the same time.

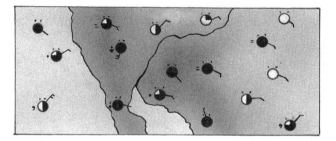

Temperature inversion. A situation which arises where a layer of warmer air lies above cooler air, making the temperature increase or stay the same, rather than decreasing, with height.

Thermal. A rising current of warm air which is caused by a local area of the Earth's surface heating up more than its surroundings.

Tornado. A violently rotating column of air which may extend from the base of a cumulonimbus cloud. It is thought to be formed by strong upward currents of air which exist within the cloud.

Tropical cyclone. A severe storm, with torrential rain and strong winds, formed over warm seas between 5° and 20° north and south of the equator. It may also be called a hurricane or a typhoon.

Warm front. The boundary between a mass of warm air and a mass of cooler air, where the warm air moves in to replace the cooler air.

Wind. Air moving from high pressure areas to areas of lower pressure.

Index

Acid rain, 41, 46
Air (atmosphere), 4-5
　-masses, 11, 12, 16, 17
　-movement (winds), 8, 9, 10, 11, 16
　-pollution, 40, 41
　-pressure, 4, 8-9, 10-11, 20, 45, 46
　-temperature, 7, 11, 42
Antarctica, 33, 36, 40, 45
Anticyclones, 16, 46
Atmosphere(s), 4, 5, 36, 37
　Earth's- 4, 5
　-on different planets, 4-5
　-pollution, 40, 41
　-pressure, 4, 46
Automatic weather stations, 24, 28

Barometer, 8, 45, 46
Beaufort scale, 45, 46
Blocking highs, 21, 46
Buys-Ballot law, 16

Carbon dioxide, 4, 38
City climates, 34
Climate(s), 32-33, 34-35, 44, 46
　change, 36-37, 38-39, 42
　city-, 34
　worldwide-, 32
Cloud(s), 12-13, 27, 43, 44
　-cover, 13, 27
　-formation, 12
　"surface"-, 15
　-types, 13, 27
Coastal (sea) fog, 15, 22, 30
Cold front, 17, 46
Computer models, 29, 42, 46
Contrails, 13
Convection, 7, 12, 46
Coriolis effect, 9, 16, 46
Cyclones, 16, 46

Depressions (low pressure areas),
　10-11, 16-17, 21, 22, 30, 43, 45
　frontal-, 17
Deserts, 32, 33, 44
Dew, 15
Dew point, 12, 15, 46
Droughts, 20, 21, 44

Floods, 20, 43
Fog, 15, 22, 28
　-in valleys, 23
　sea (coastal)-, 15, 22, 30
Forecasts, 30-31
Fronts, 16-17, 30, 46,
　cold-, 17, 46
　occluded-, 17
　polar-, 16
　warm-, 17, 47
Frontal depressions, 17
Frost, 15, 23

General circulation models, 42
Geostationary satellites, 25, 30, 46
Global warming, 38-39, 42, 46
Greenhouse effect, 38, 46
Greenhouse gases, 38, 39, 46
Grid points, 29

Hail, 14, 28
High-level winds, 10, 17, 19, 21, 24
High pressure areas, 8-9, 10-11, 16,
　20, 21, 22, 30, 44, 45
　blocking-, 21
Humidity, 11, 12, 21, 27, 29, 46
Hurricanes, 3, 18-19, 43, 47

Ice, 7, 14, 39, 42
　-crystals, 12, 13, 14, 15
Ice ages, 36, 37, 46
Intertropical Convergence Zone
(ITCZ), 9, 20, 46
Isobars, 16, 46

Jet streams, 10, 21, 47

Land breezes, 22
Light energy, 23
Lightning, 18
Low pressure areas, 8-9, 10-11, 16-17,
　21, 22, 30, 43, 45

Mist, 15, 28
Moon, 5
Monsoons, 20, 21, 32, 47

Observations, 24-25, 26-27, 28, 29
Occluded fronts, 17, 47
Ocean (sea) currents, 19, 22
Overgrazing, 20
Ozone gas, 4, 5, 40
　surface-, 40
Ozone layer, 5, 40, 47

Photochemical smog, 40
Polar climate, 32
Polar orbiting satellite, 5, 25, 47
Pollution, 40-41
Precipitation, 12, 14, 27, 29, 47
Pressure, 4, 8-9, 10, 11, 16, 17, 19, 22,
　24, 27, 28, 29
　-differences, 8-9, 10, 11, 16
　-extremes, 20, 45
　-at fronts 16-17
Prevailing wind, 22, 47

Radars, 25
Radiosondes, 24, 47
Rain, 12, 13, 14, 15, 25, 29, 32, 33, 44
　acid-, 41
　-forests, 33
　-shadows, 44
Rainbows, 23

Satellite(s), 5, 25
　hurricane detection, 19
　geostationary-, 25, 30, 46
　-images, 19, 25, 28, 30, 31
　polar orbiting-, 5, 25, 47
Sea breezes, 22
Sea (coastal) fog, 15, 22, 30
Seasons, 6
Sleet, 14
Smog, 40, 47
　photochemical-, 40
Snow, 7, 14, 28, 29, 30, 45
Solar radiation (energy), 4, 6-7, 9, 12,
　22, 23, 33, 35, 36, 37, 38, 40, 42,
　43, 44, 45
Solar System, 4
Storm(s), 18, 19, 43, 45
　-surge, 43
Stratosphere, 4, 5, 40
Sun, 4, 6-7, 45
Surface temperature, 7, 11
Synoptic charts, 28, 29, 47

Temperature, 22, 26, 28, 44, 45
　body-, 35
　-extremes. 20, 44, 45
　-increase, 38, 39, 42, 43
　-inversions, 40, 47
　sea-, 39, 43
Thermals, 7, 44, 47
Thunder, 13, 18
Thunderstorms, 18, 28
Tornado, 45, 47
Tropical climates, 12, 32, 33, 34
Tropical cyclones, 3, 18, 47
Typhoons, 18, 45, 47

Valley winds, 23
Visibility, 15, 27
Volcanoes, 36, 37

Warm front, 17, 47
Water vapor, 11, 12, 19, 20, 21
Weather forecasts, 30-31
Weather observations, 24-25, 26-27
Weather stations, 24, 26-27, 28
Wind(s), 8, 9, 10-11, 29, 47
　-chill factor, 35
　high-level-, 10, 17, 19, 21
　-around highs and lows, 16, 17
　hurricane-, 19, 43
　seasonal-, 20
　valley-, 23
　world's main- 9

BOOK TWO
ENERGY & POWER

Richard Spurgeon and Mike Flood

Edited by Corinne Stockley

Designed by Stephen Wright

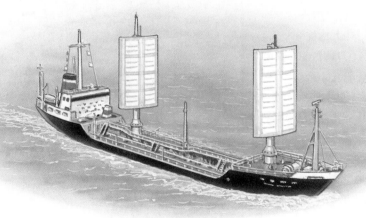

Illustrated by Kuo Kang Chen and Joseph McEwan

Additional designs by Christopher Gillingwater

Contents

51 About this book
52 What is energy?
54 Energy changes
56 Stored energy
58 Movement energy
60 Electricity
62 Energy and the earth
64 The coal industry
66 Oil and gas
68 Nuclear power
70 The electricity industry
72 Making an electromagnet
73 Renewable energy/Solar energy
75 More solar projects
76 Energy from plants
78 Wind energy
80 Energy from water
82 Energy efficiency
84 Efficiency in industry
85 Efficiency in transportation
86 Energy in the future
88 World energy facts
92 The economics of energy
93 Further information
94 Glossary
96 Index

USBORNE SCIENCE & EXPERIMENTS

About this book

Energy is vital to the world and all the people who live in it. This book explains all about energy and how it is related to power. It looks at all the different forms of energy and how we use them in our daily lives.

There are sections on both traditional sources of energy, such as coal and oil, and also renewable sources, such as the sun and the wind. The book also looks at problems linked with producing energy, for example, the damage caused to the environment by burning fossil fuels, and the unbalanced use of energy around the world. It also examines ways in which we can secure enough energy for the future.

Using the glossary

The glossary on pages 94-95 is a useful reference point. It explains all the more complex terms in the book, as well as introducing some new related words.

Useful addresses

On page 93 there is a list of some of the groups, associations and other organizations you could write to if you want to learn more about energy and power. They will be able to provide you with written material which you can use for projects, and also possibly other addresses you could write to.

Activities and projects

Special boxes like this one are found throughout the main section of the book. They are used for simple activities and experiments which will help you to understand the scientific ideas and principles behind the production and use of energy. All these activities have clear instructions and are easy to do. They all use basic materials.

This scene shows a hydro-electric power station with its enormous dam. It makes use of moving water to turn turbines and produce electricity. The movement energy turns into electrical energy. For more about hydro-electricity, see pages 80-81.

What is energy?

Everything that changes or moves has some form of energy. People depend on energy in many ways — it is what makes things happen. It is used all around us, in transportation, in industry and in the home. On these pages, you can find out much more about what energy is and how it behaves.

Below are a few examples of different forms of energy being produced or used. You can find out more about them on pages 54-61.

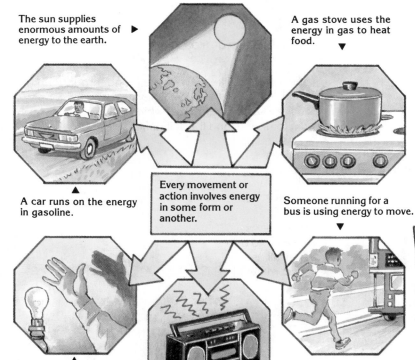

The sun supplies enormous amounts of energy to the earth. ▶

A gas stove uses the energy in gas to heat food. ▼

▲ A car runs on the energy in gasoline.

Every movement or action involves energy in some form or another.

Someone running for a bus is using energy to move. ▼

A light bulb uses electrical energy to produce light.

◀ Sound from a radio is a form of energy.

Stored energy

Energy makes things move or change. The energy in moving things is called kinetic energy. But energy can also be stored in many different things and in a number of different ways. For example, there is a lot of energy stored in things such as wood and coal, and also in food. This energy is locked up in the chemical make-up of the substance, and can only be released when this chemical make-up changes. It is called chemical energy.

Stored energy is released when wood is burned.

Wood (a good source of stored chemical energy)   Ash

Burning the wood changes its chemical make-up, releasing some of the chemical energy as heat energy (for more about energy changes, see pages 54-55).

People depend on stored energy. Without energy from our food, we could do nothing, not even breathe. Without fuels like wood, coal or gas, most people could not cook or keep warm, industries would not work, and cars, trains and airplanes would not move.

Energy is also stored in coiled-up springs and stretched rubber bands. In this form, it is called strain energy. For more about this, see page 57.

The coiled spring at the base of the toy has stored energy (strain energy).

When the spring expands, the energy is released as kinetic (movement) energy.

Energy and your body

At this moment, you are using energy in many different ways. You are using light to read this book and heat to keep warm. You are also using energy to stay alive. Without the energy you get from the food you eat, your body would not be able to work. Actions like breathing and the pumping of blood around your body depend on energy.

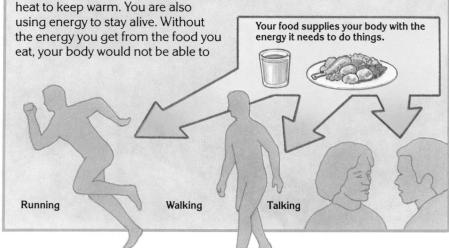

Your food supplies your body with the energy it needs to do things.

Running   Walking   Talking

52

Measuring energy

Energy is normally measured in very small units called joules (J)*. A thousand joules is a kilojoule (kJ). An ordinary-sized apple (3½oz), for example, contains 150kJ. The same weight of milk chocolate will provide over 15 times as much energy (2,335kJ). Eating too much high-energy food, like chocolate, may lead to health problems. Try to find out how much energy there is in the food you eat. Often the number of kilojoules that a type of food contains is written on the tin, box or wrapper.

Each 100kJ you eat will allow you to:

walk quickly for 5 minutes

cycle for 3 minutes

jog for 2 minutes

sleep for half an hour

Power

Heat from the coal boiled water to make steam, which powered the engine.

Coal was burned in the fire-box of the steam engine.

The terms "power" and "energy" are often confused. In the scientific world, the word "power" means only one thing, that is, the rate (how fast) energy is produced or used. Machines are used to turn one form of energy into a different form (for more about energy changes, see pages 54-55). For example, an old-style steam engine turned the chemical energy in coal into movement.

The more energy a machine uses in a certain period of time, the more powerful it is, and the more energy it can provide. A two-bar electric heater is twice as powerful as a single-bar heater. Over the same period of time, it will provide twice as much energy.

The power of a single-bar heater is equivalent to that of seven strong people working very hard.

Measuring power

Power is measured in units called watts (W). A thousand watts make up a kilowatt (kW). Power is the measurement of energy used up in a certain time. One watt is equal to one joule per second. For instance, a 60 watt light bulb uses 60 joules (J) of energy each second (s).

Some appliances are used for longer periods than others. An electric iron is used on average for 20 minutes a day, whereas a television might be on for five hours. The energy used (J) equals the power of the appliance (W), times the number of seconds it is used for (s).

$$1W = 1J/s$$

$$J = W \times s$$

Below are the power ratings of some household appliances.

Electric iron 1000W

Portable radio 10W

Microwave oven 650W

Washing machine 2500W

A matchbox paddle-boat

You can make a tiny paddle-boat with two used matches, two empty matchboxes and a small, thin rubber band.

Place the two matches into the sides of one empty matchbox, pointing slightly downwards. Attach the rubber band loosely between the matches.

Rubber band

Cut one end off the other matchbox tray, slide it into the rubber band and twist it, so that it winds up the rubber band. Place it in some water and watch it go.

Energy stored in the twisted rubber band is released to turn the paddle and make the boat move forward. This is an example of an energy change (see pages 54-55). The energy changes from strain energy to moving, or kinetic, energy.

You may have to trim the paddle so it can spin all the way around.

Energy changes

Energy exists in many different forms – the main ones are shown here. When something happens, energy is always involved. One form of energy changes into one or more other forms. For example, a battery, when connected up, changes chemical energy into electrical energy (see below).

Forms of energy

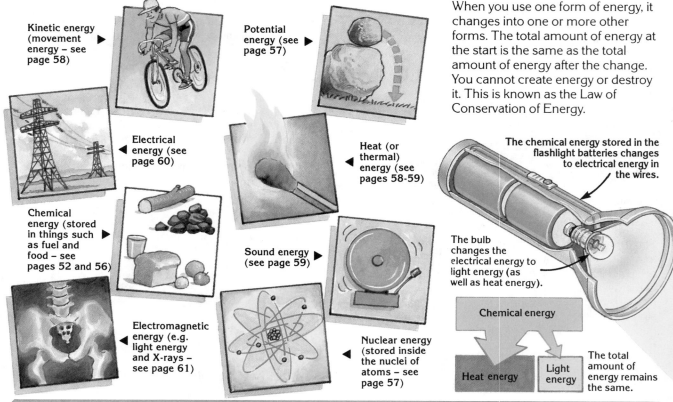

Kinetic energy (movement energy – see page 58) ▶

Potential energy (see page 57) ▶

◀ Electrical energy (see page 60)

◀ Heat (or thermal) energy (see pages 58-59)

Chemical energy (stored in things such as fuel and food – see pages 52 and 56) ▶

Sound energy (see page 59) ▶

Electromagnetic energy (e.g. light energy and X-rays – see page 61) ▶

◀ Nuclear energy (stored inside the nuclei of atoms – see page 57)

Conservation of energy

When you use one form of energy, it changes into one or more other forms. The total amount of energy at the start is the same as the total amount of energy after the change. You cannot create energy or destroy it. This is known as the Law of Conservation of Energy.

The chemical energy stored in the flashlight batteries changes to electrical energy in the wires.

The bulb changes the electrical energy to light energy (as well as heat energy).

Chemical energy

Heat energy

Light energy

The total amount of energy remains the same.

A funnel record player

Old-fashioned record players show an example of a simple energy change. The loudspeakers on these record players were much less complicated than those of today. You can make something similar using a paper funnel and a needle. You will also need an old, unwanted record and the use of a turntable.

Roll a large, square piece of thin cardboard into a funnel and tape it together.

Push the needle through the cardboard at an angle. It should be 1-1½ in from the end.

Hold the funnel as still as you can. You should be able to hear the music.

Put the record on the turntable at the right speed. Then place the point of the needle in the groove, making sure that it is pointing the right way (in the direction the record is turning).

Tiny marks in the record's groove make the needle vibrate as it passes over them. The needle passes on the vibrations to the air inside the funnel, producing sound waves. The shape of the funnel concentrates these waves so the sound can be heard more clearly.

The vibrations of the needle make the paper funnel vibrate (kinetic energy), which creates wave patterns in the air (sound energy).

Energy efficiency

The Law of Conservation of Energy states that energy cannot be created or destroyed. However, when energy changes from one form to another, some energy is "lost," that is, it is changed into other forms of energy that may not be wanted.

A light bulb turns electrical energy into light energy. However, a lot of energy is "lost" as heat energy, which is probably not needed.

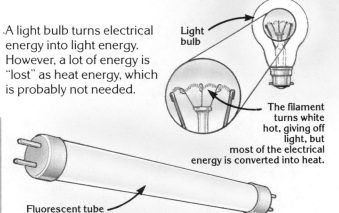

Light bulb

The filament turns white hot, giving off light, but most of the electrical energy is converted into heat.

Fluorescent tube

Energy chains

Energy chains are an easy way to show how energy can change from one form to another, perhaps several times. They can also show how energy is "lost" along the chain. Because of this energy "loss," the amount of useful energy passed on along the chain gets less and less. An example of an energy chain is given below.

Nuclear reactions inside the sun release enormous amounts of energy, some of which travel across space in the form of light (see pages 61 and 62).

Plants use some of the sun's light energy to make their own food (containing chemical energy), which is stored in the plant. Some energy is also used by the plant for its own growth.

When people eat plants, they create their own store of chemical energy. Some of this is used to keep their bodies working, for example, for breathing and moving (kinetic energy). Some is "lost" as body heat.

The kinetic energy used in winding up an alarm clock changes into strain energy in the spring of the clock. Some energy is "lost," due to friction in the moving parts of the clock.

When the alarm goes off, the strain energy changes into mechanical energy (in the hammer). The vibration of the bells produces sound energy. Some energy is "lost," due to friction.

Nuclear energy

Light energy

Chemical energy

Kinetic energy   Strain energy

Sound energy

Machines and appliances are described as efficient if they change most of their energy into the useful form of energy that is needed. For example, fluorescent tube lights are more efficient than normal light bulbs, because they turn more of the electrical energy into light and "waste" less as heat. For more about energy efficiency, see pages 82-85.

Friction is another cause of energy "loss." It is the resistance between two objects when they come into contact with each other, or the resistance between a moving object and the air moving past it.

Friction changes kinetic (movement) energy into heat and sound energy. For example, a car moving on flat ground with its engine off will gradually slow down and stop due to friction.

Friction between the car and the air

Friction between the wheels and the ground

A small amount of energy is "lost" as sound (the noise that the car makes).

Energy is "lost" as heat (in all the places that there is friction).

The less friction there is, the less energy is "lost" and the more efficient the car is (the further it will go on a certain amount of gas).

Friction between the moving parts of the car

Stored energy

The forms of energy on these two pages are all types of stored energy, that is, they are all "hidden," or latent, energy. Under certain conditions, they can all change into other forms of energy (for more about energy changes, see pages 54-55).

Atomic structure

Everything around you is made up of "building blocks" called atoms, which are far too small for the eye to see. In most everyday things there are billions of atoms, yet atoms themselves are made up of much smaller things (subatomic particles) called protons, neutrons and electrons.

Nucleus

Electron

Proton

Neutron

Simple model of an atom

Simple model of a water molecule

Hydrogen atom

Oxygen atom

A molecule is a group of atoms joined (bonded) together. For example, a water molecule is made of two hydrogen atoms and one oxygen atom. Atoms and molecules are important in stored energy.

Chemical energy

Chemical energy is the energy stored in the chemical make-up of certain substances. It is stored in the bonds between the atoms in their molecules. When these bonds are broken (for example, when a substance burns), some of this energy is released as heat and light.

For example, every methane molecule in natural gas is made up of one carbon atom and four hydrogen atoms. When the gas is burned in air, the methane molecules break apart. The stored energy is released as light and heat energy. The carbon and hydrogen atoms combine with oxygen in the air to form water and carbon dioxide.

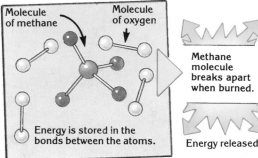

Molecule of methane

Molecule of oxygen

Energy is stored in the bonds between the atoms.

Methane molecule breaks apart when burned.

Energy released

Molecule of water

Molecule of carbon dioxide

Fuels

A fuel is something that can release heat energy. Some common examples of fuels are wood, coal, oil and gas. Fuels are used in the home and, in much greater amounts, in power stations (see pages 70-71). The food we eat is also a kind of fuel – it is "burned up" inside our bodies to provide us with energy.

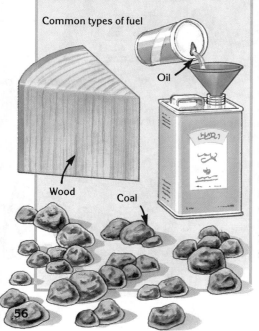

Common types of fuel

Oil

Wood

Coal

Wood, coal and oil have more complex chemical structures than natural gas, but they burn in a similar way, producing carbon dioxide and water vapour. They also produce more waste products because they are impure (they contain other substances as well as carbon and hydrogen). Coal, for example, produces ash and gases such as sulphur dioxide due to minerals it contains.

Because of their different chemical structures, a certain amount of one fuel will give off more heat than the same amount of another. A certain amount of natural gas gives off more heat than the same amount of oil, and oil gives off more heat than coal.

Power stations using coal and oil produce a lot of pollution.

Sulphur dioxide

Nitrogen oxides

Carbon dioxide

The waste gases they release into the air are partly to blame for environmental problems like acid rain and the greenhouse effect (see page 65).

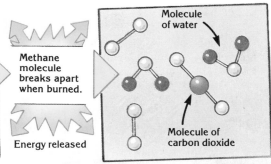

Water vapor

Make your own battery

A battery is a store of chemical energy. The stored energy turns into electrical energy when the battery is used. Inside the casing, different chemicals are stored which react together to create an electrical current.

You can make your own battery using some very basic things. You need one copper-coated and one zinc-coated (galvanized) nail, some thin, insulated wire (about 20 in), a compass and a container of salty water or watered-down vinegar.

To measure the small electric current that you will produce, you need to coil the wire as many times as you can around the compass, to make a simple meter (you should be able to make more coils than are shown here). Leave some wire at each end.

Attach the compass to a flat surface, making sure the pointer is lined up with the coiled wire.

Strip the insulation from the ends of the wire. Ask someone if you are not sure how to do this.

Tape

Bare ends of the wire

Twist and tape the bare ends around the two nails.

Put the nails into the container with the salty water or vinegar.

Watch out for movement in the compass needle. This shows if any electrical energy is being produced.

The reaction which takes place in the chemicals (salt or vinegar) in solution releases electrical energy. This flows through the wire, creating a magnetic field which causes the needle to move.

Try putting the nails into a lemon, a potato, a glass of fizzy drink — in fact, try lots of different things. Which makes the best home-made battery?

Strain energy

Strain energy is another form of stored energy (see also page 52). It results from stretching or compressing an object, and is the energy an object has because it is "trying" to return to its former shape.

When you wind up a clockwork watch, you are storing strain energy in its spring.

The energy in the stretched (or compressed) spring is slowly released as kinetic (movement) energy to move the wheels and cogs of the watch.

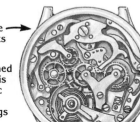

Nuclear energy

Nuclear energy is another kind of stored energy. It comes from the energy that holds together the tiny particles (protons and neutrons) in the nucleus of an atom. There are two ways of releasing this energy: fission and fusion.

Fission

Nucleus of heavy atom (uranium or plutonium) breaks apart, releasing enormous amounts of energy.

This happens inside a nuclear reactor at a nuclear power station, and when a fission, or atom ("A"), bomb explodes.

Fusion

Small nuclei (e.g. those of deuterium and tritium) fuse (join) together, releasing vast amounts of energy.

This is happening all the time in the sun. It also happens when the most powerful nuclear weapon, a fusion, or hydrogen ("H"), bomb explodes.

Potential energy

Potential energy is the energy that an object has because of its position in some kind of force field, such as a gravitational or magnetic field. The example below shows a set of events involving two different forms of potential energy, one caused by gravity, the other caused by a magnet.

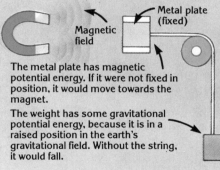

Magnetic field

Metal plate (fixed)

The metal plate has magnetic potential energy. If it were not fixed in position, it would move towards the magnet.

The weight has some gravitational potential energy, because it is in a raised position in the earth's gravitational field. Without the string, it would fall.

When the plate is detached and free to move, it is drawn towards the magnet by the magnetic field. It does a job of work against the earth's gravitational field by lifting the string and weight.

The weight now has more gravitational potential energy (it is higher up).

When the magnet is taken away, the gravitational potential energy of the weight turns into kinetic (movement) energy as it falls back down.

For more about gravitational potential energy and kinetic energy, see page 58.

57

Movement energy

The energy contained in any moving object is called kinetic energy (also known as movement or motion energy). Many forms of energy are based in some way on kinetic energy. The main ones are described on these two pages.

A moving bicycle has kinetic energy.

A car moving at the same speed as the bicycle has more kinetic energy.

The greater the mass of the object, the more kinetic energy it has when moving at a given speed.

An arrow is small and light, but it has a lot of kinetic energy because it travels very fast.

The faster an object travels, the greater its kinetic energy.

Mechanical energy

Mechanical energy is a term that is used to describe several different types of energy. For example, it covers both kinetic energy and gravitational potential energy, and the combination of the two (see below).

A rock balanced on the edge of a cliff has gravitational potential energy because of its position (see page 57). It is capable of doing work.

If it is attached by a rope to an object, using a pulley system, the rock will lift the object some distance when it is pushed over the edge.

Pulley system

Rock

Object

When this happens, the rock's gravitational potential energy will change into kinetic energy and the rock's speed will increase:

As it begins to fall, it has mainly potential energy, and a small amount of kinetic energy.

Lower down, more of the gravitational potential energy has changed into kinetic energy, as the rock has speeded up on its way down.

Just before it hits the ground, it has very little gravitational potential energy and a lot of kinetic energy.

At all times, its mechanical energy remains the same, but its form changes from gravitational potential to kinetic energy.

Heat energy

Heat energy is closely connected to kinetic energy, as it is the energy which causes the atoms and molecules of a substance to vibrate (move around). When a substance is heated, its atoms or molecules begin to vibrate more vigorously. When it cools down, its atoms or molecules vibrate more slowly. Heat energy flows from hot objects to cold ones and continues to flow until they are the same temperature.

Heat and temperature

Temperature can be thought of as a measure of the vibration of the atoms or molecules of a substance. However, the amount of vibration caused by a certain amount of heat is different for each substance. If you add equal amounts of heat to identical amounts of two different substances, they will end up with different temperatures. Different substances are said to have different thermal capacities.

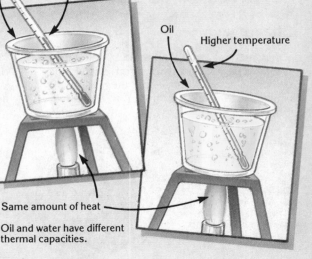

Water

Lower temperature

Oil

Higher temperature

Same amount of heat

Oil and water have different thermal capacities.

Temperature is the measure of how hot something is, and is measured in degrees Celsius (°C) or Fahrenheit (°F). The amount of heat energy an object can possess is related to its temperature, but also to other factors, such as its size and density.

A red-hot needle has a high temperature, but does not have much heat energy. If it is dropped into a bowl of cold water, there is very little change in the water's temperature, because the needle is so small. A larger object of the same temperature would heat up the water more, because it possesses more heat energy.

Heat energy is measured in joules (J). It takes 4.2J to raise the temperature of 1g (0.035oz) of water by 1°C. To heat 10g (0.35oz) of water from room temperature (16°C) to boiling point (100°C) takes 3,528J.

Conduction is a way in which heat energy travels in solids and liquids. Heat spreads when the vibration of one atom or molecule is passed on to the next. Some materials, such as iron and copper, allow heat to flow through them easily and are called conductors (they conduct heat well). Others, such as wood and expanded Styrofoam, do not allow an easy flow, and are called insulators (they are bad conductors).

Metals such as copper are often used for making pots and pans, as they are good conductors of heat. The heat from the stove reaches the food quickly.

Wooden handles and spoons are insulators. They stop the heat from reaching your hands.

Convection is another way in which heat energy can be transferred. When the atoms or molecules of a liquid or gas are heated, they gain more energy and so move more quickly and further apart. The heated liquid or gas expands and becomes less dense. It is lighter, so moves upwards, away from the heat source. The colder, more dense liquid or gas moves down.

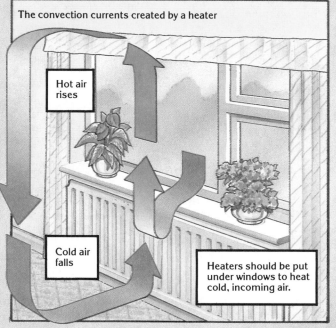

The convection currents created by a heater

Hot air rises

Cold air falls

Heaters should be put under windows to heat cold, incoming air.

Radiation is a third way in which heat energy can be transferred. The heat energy travels in the form of electromagnetic waves, mainly infra-red radiation (see page 61). Radiation does not depend on the movement of atoms or molecules, so this energy is the only form of energy that can travel across a vacuum (for example, through space).

A heat-sensitive spiral

A cardboard spiral can be used to show the convection currents of air above a heat source. The energy in the moving air makes the spiral turn.

Cut out a large circle from thin cardboard, and draw a line in the shape of a spiral. The gaps between the lines should be about ½ in wide. You could decorate the spiral with a brightly colored design.

Carefully make a tiny hole in the center. Push a long piece of cotton through and tie a knot underneath.

Cut along the spiral with some sharp scissors (be careful how you use these).

Hang the spiral over a heater and watch what happens.

Convection currents are almost invisible, but you can sometimes see them (as a "shaky" effect in the air) above a very hot fire, or above the ground on a very hot day.

The mechanical equivalent of heat

In the 1840's, the scientist Joule worked out the connection between heat and mechanical energy. Using a machine like the one shown here, he measured how much mechanical energy (in the falling weights) was needed to raise the temperature of the water by a certain amount (by stirring it).

Handle   Pulley

Copper cylinder

Water

Falling weights made the paddles turn, causing the water to swirl about and heat up.

Sound energy

Some opera singers can shatter a glass with the sound of their voice. This shows that sound is a form of energy (because energy makes sound waves move).

The sound of the singer's voice sets off a wave which travels through the air.

As the sound wave moves, particles in the air knock into each other, passing on the energy. These particles have kinetic energy.

The glass resonates with the energy of the sound (the molecules in the glass vibrate at the same rate as the molecules in the air), causing it to crack.

Electricity

We use electricity, or electrical energy, all the time in our daily lives (for more about how it is produced, see pages 70-71). It powers many different appliances, such as irons and stoves, and it can also give us heat and light by making metal wires glow, for example in electric heaters or the filaments of light bulbs. The way electricity behaves is connected with the behavior of the tiny particles called electrons which form part of atoms (see page 56).

Static electricity

Static electricity is the electricity "held" in an object which has an electrical charge. An object has an electrical charge if its atoms have more or fewer electrons than atoms of the same substance would normally have. Most objects have no charge because their atoms have the normal number of electrons. But if they gain or lose electrons, they become charged, and can then attract or repel other objects.

If you rub a balloon against your clothing, you can make it stick to the wall or ceiling.

This is because the rubber in the balloon becomes charged with static electricity, and is attracted to the wall.

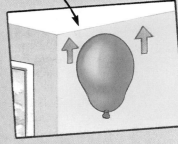

An electrical charge builds up in the base of a cloud.

The flash of lightning is a very powerful electrical spark.

◄ Lightning is a result of static electricity. Water molecules in a cloud rub together with air molecules, creating an electrical charge in the base of the cloud. This is attracted to the earth and the charge (electrons) is released as a flash of lightning.

Current electricity

You can think of an electric current as a flow of electrons. It is measured in amperes, or amps (A). The electrons flow because a force acts on them (an electromotive force, or emf). This force is measured in volts (V).

It is sometimes useful to compare the behavior of electricity in a wire with that of water in a pipe.

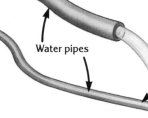

Water pipes

Electricity flows when a force is applied, e.g. from a battery. Water in a pipe also needs a force, e.g. from a water pump.

The thinner the wire (or pipe), the harder it is for the electrons (or water) to flow through it.

Electricity travels most easily through metals, such as copper and iron. These are called conductors. It can also pass through water or, if the force is powerful enough, through air as a spark (as in lightning). Some things, such as plastic and rubber, slow down the electrical flow, and are called insulators.

The amount of power (the rate of flow of electricity) is related to the size of the current and the electromotive force. If an emf of one volt causes a current of one amp to flow through a wire, it will produce one watt of power.

Copper is the metal most often used in electrical wires.

The wires are covered in plastic, which insulates them, making them safe to touch.

$$W = V \times A$$

W = power in watts

V = electromotive force in volts

A = current in amps

Storing electricity

It is very expensive and difficult to store electricity as electricity. Instead, it is almost always changed into another form of energy for storage. For example, batteries are used to store electricity (as chemical energy – see page 57). Another way is to use the electricity to drive a device called a flywheel. The energy is "stored" as mechanical energy.

The current makes the flywheel turn very quickly, turning electricity into mechanical energy.

Some of the energy stored in the flywheel can be turned back into electricity using a generator.

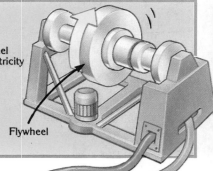

Flywheel

Electromagnetic energy

Electromagnetic energy can be thought of as a combination of electricity and magnetism (magnetic energy). It travels in the form of regular wave patterns. The electromagnetic spectrum is the range of the different, related forms of electromagnetic energy. These have different wavelengths and frequencies (see right and below).

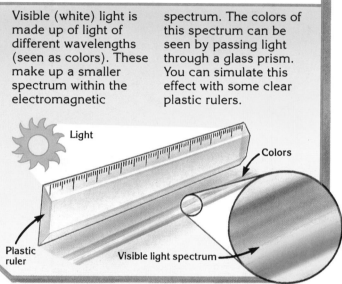

The wavelength is the distance over which the wave pattern repeats itself.

The frequency is the number of waves that occur in one second. It is the number of wavelengths per second.

Wave

The electromagnetic spectrum

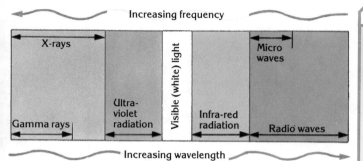

Increasing frequency

X-rays

Gamma rays

Ultra-violet radiation

Visible (white) light

Infra-red radiation

Micro waves

Radio waves

Increasing wavelength

Without the different kinds of electromagnetic energy from the sun (ultra-violet radiation, visible light and infra-red radiation), there would be no life on earth. The sun provides us with light and heat, as well as supplying plants, the basis of life on earth, with the energy they need to grow (see pages 62-63).

The other forms of electromagnetic energy are very useful, too. For example, radio waves are used to communicate over long and short distances. Microwaves are a particular kind of radio wave, and are used in radar (RAdio Detection And Ranging). They are also used in microwave ovens to cook food.

Splitting the spectrum

Visible (white) light is made up of light of different wavelengths (seen as colors). These make up a smaller spectrum within the electromagnetic spectrum. The colors of this spectrum can be seen by passing light through a glass prism. You can simulate this effect with some clear plastic rulers.

Light

Colors

Plastic ruler

Visible light spectrum

The quality of energy

Some forms of energy are more useful than others — they can be used to do a large number of things, and do them more efficiently. These more useful forms of energy are said to be of a higher quality. For example, electricity is a much higher quality form of energy than low temperature heat energy. It can be used for many more things, such as powering appliances and producing light.

High quality forms of energy can be changed into other forms of energy (for example, electricity into heat) very efficiently, that is, without losing much energy in the process. But changing low or medium quality energy into high quality energy is very inefficient and wasteful (see below and right).

Power stations turn hot steam (a medium quality energy) into electricity (a high quality energy).

This is very inefficient — two-thirds of the energy is lost as heat.

In this case, heat is lost in water vapor.

Radar works out the position of an object by sending out microwaves and timing how long it takes for them to come back after being reflected off the object.

Infra-red radiation can be used to make thermal images. These are similar to photographs, except that variations in heat, rather than light, are used to record the image.

Thermal image of heat loss from a house

X-ray image

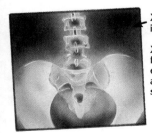

X-rays are used to show breaks and fractures in bones. The rays pass more easily through flesh than through bone, and record an image of the bone on special photographic plates.

Energy and the earth

The sun produces tremendous amounts of energy, which streams into space in all directions. Some of this energy is captured by the earth. It is what makes life possible on our planet – without it, the earth would be a frozen mass of ice and rock, and no living thing would survive.

The sun's energy reaches the earth in the form of electromagnetic energy (see page 61), the only form of energy that can travel across space. Most of this energy reaches the earth as infra-red and ultra-violet radiation, and visible light. The many uses of this solar energy are described on pages 73-75.

The sun produces 400 million million million million watts of power.

The sun is about 93 million miles away, and its mass is one third of a million times greater than that of the earth.

Nuclear fusion (see page 57) takes place in the core of the sun, where the temperature can reach 57,000,000°F. This releases vast amounts of energy.

The amount of energy the earth receives from the sun is the equivalent of the energy supplied by over 100 million large power stations.

Energy in water

Water covers 70% of the earth's surface, and is vital to all living things. It is continuously circulating, in the water cycle, between the surface and the atmosphere, driven by the sun's energy. There is a lot of energy contained in the movement of water. This has been used for hundreds of years, for example in water mills. Today, it is widely used to produce electricity in hydro-electric power stations (for more about this, see pages 80-81).

The water cycle

Heat from the sun makes water evaporate from the surface of the land and sea, forming water vapor.

As the air rises, it cools. The water vapor begins to condense (become liquid again), forming masses of small droplets (clouds).

Energy in the wind

More of the sun's energy falls at the equator than at the poles, so the equatorial regions are much hotter. As it is heated, the air in these regions expands and rises, and colder, denser air rushes in. These air movements cause winds all over the world and influence weather patterns.

Patterns of air movements or winds ▶

The same amount of the sun's energy is spread over a larger area at the poles than at the equator.

Heated air rises (up to 8 mi above the surface), flows north and south, cools and sinks.

Some air flows back to the equator, some flows to the polar areas.

Cold air flows away from the polar regions.

North pole

Equator

South pole

The flow of the air masses is affected by the rotation of the earth.

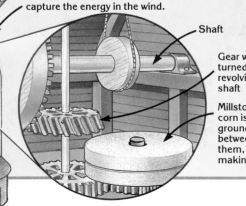

Blades

Windmills have been used for centuries to capture the energy in the wind.

Shaft

Gear wheels, turned by the revolving shaft

Millstones — corn is ground between them, making flour.

The energy of the wind has been used by people for hundreds of years, for example to sail boats, pump water and grind corn. It is now used more and more to produce electricity. For more about wind power, see pages 78-79.

Wherever the wind blows over water, some of its energy goes into creating waves. So these, too, are indirectly produced by the energy of the sun. The energy in waves is one example of the energy in water (see above and right).

As the clouds cool further, the water droplets get bigger. Finally, they fall as rain or snow.

Moving water in rivers has a lot of kinetic energy.

The energy of moving water in rivers is used in hydro-electric power stations. Another type of energy in water is wave energy. You can find out more on page 80 about how this could be used to produce electricity. It may also be possible in the future to produce energy by using the temperature difference between the top and lower layers of water in the oceans (see page 81).

The constant rising and falling of the tides is now also being used to produce electricity. For more about this, see page 80.

Tides are caused by the pull of the moon's gravity and the spinning of the earth.

These create two bulges in the water of the oceans, with troughs (low points) in between.

As these bulges and troughs travel around the earth once a day, they raise and lower the levels of the seas and oceans, creating high and low tides.

The effects of the tides are very slight in mid-ocean, but they are very noticeable on the shores, and especially obvious in bays and river estuaries.

Energy in plants

All green plants take in the sun's energy, as part of a process called photosynthesis, in order to make their own food. This is stored as chemical energy, and used ("burned") to give the plants energy to grow.

If plants are burned, the stored chemical energy can be turned into useful heat energy. Fast-growing trees and other plants can provide a great deal of energy in this way (see page 77).

The sun's energy is changed into chemical energy stored in the plant.

When the plant is eaten by an animal, this chemical energy is stored in the animal's body, and then used to keep it alive.

Coal, oil and gas are known as fossil fuels because they are the remains of plants and animals that lived millions of years ago. They are vast stores of chemical energy. Without them, our modern way of life would not be possible. For more about them, see pages 64-67.

The formation of coal (a fossil fuel)

Plants grew millions of years ago. In swamps, they sank to the bottom when they died and did not rot (as there was no air).

Over millions of years, other layers formed on top.

Plant matter turned to coal under pressure.

This is now brought up and used as fuel.

Energy in the earth

The earth itself is a store of an enormous amount of heat energy. This can be seen in volcanic activity, when molten rock (so hot it has become liquid) is pushed up through the earth's crust.

For many years, people in countries such as Iceland, Japan and New Zealand have used steam and hot water coming up from the earth to provide them with heating. These energy sources are now used on a larger scale (see page 81).

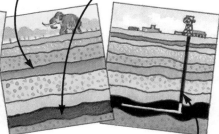

Active volcano

Molten rock, called lava

The layers of the earth (see below) get hotter going down. The inner core is thought to have a temperature of about 6,700°F.

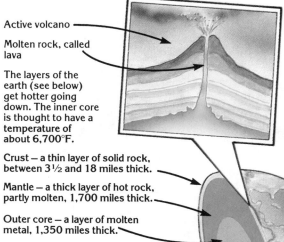

Crust — a thin layer of solid rock, between 3½ and 18 miles thick.

Mantle — a thick layer of hot rock, partly molten, 1,700 miles thick.

Outer core — a layer of molten metal, 1,350 miles thick.

Inner core — thought to be a ball of solid metal, 1,500 miles thick.

The coal industry

Coal is a fossil fuel, formed from plant matter that grew millions of years ago. It is burned to supply heat energy and, indirectly, electricity (see pages 70-71). Coal is found in many parts of the world, but most is found in the northern half (mainly in China, the former USSR, Europe and North America – see page 91).

About 20% of the world's energy comes from coal, and its use is increasing. There are enough reserves to make it an important source of energy for another 200-300 years, but the way we use it at present causes serious environmental problems.

Modern coal mines

There are three main types of coal mine – shaft mines (underground, connected to the surface by vertical shafts), drift mines (underground, connected to the surface by sloping tunnels) and open cast mines (on the surface).

Modern shaft coal mine

The history of coal mining

Coal has been dug out and used for thousands of years. The first real mines (called bell pits because of their shape) were dug in Great Britain in the 12th century.

Early bell pit

The coal was raised using pulley systems or carried up ladders on people's backs.

These pits were never much more than 40 feet deep.

As the demand for coal grew, so did the depth and size of coal mines. This led to advances in mining technology, as problems such as cave-ins and flooding had to be overcome. During the Industrial Revolution in Europe in the 1800's, mining methods improved and more coal was produced.

Coalfaces are often several hundred feet below the surface.

Underground train system carries workers around mine.

One coalface can produce 2,200 tons of coal a day.

Coal cutter moves up and down, and along coalface.

Tunnelling machine cuts new roadway, so cutting machine can get to new coalface.

Water cools cutter and dampens down coal dust.

Steel roof supports move into coalface as coal is cut (roof falls in behind them).

Studying coal

Find several pieces of coal and inspect them very closely, using a magnifying glass if you have one. Break a piece in half and look inside. You will find that some types of coal break more easily than others, and you should be able to spot evidence of the plants the coal was formed from.

Split piece of coal

You might find tiny, whole fossilized plants.

There are different types of coal, some soft, others hard. They all contain different amounts of impurities (other substances, such as metal ores or sulphur).

Using coal

Coal is used throughout the world to produce energy. Many power stations burn coal to produce electricity – the heat from the burning coal turns water into steam to drive the turbines (see pages 70-71). Many industries, such as the steel industry, burn coal to heat their furnaces. They also burn other coal-based fuels, such as coke. Coal and coke are also burned in some homes to provide heat and hot water.

Piece of coal

Piece of coke

Coke is made by heating coal to high temperatures without air.

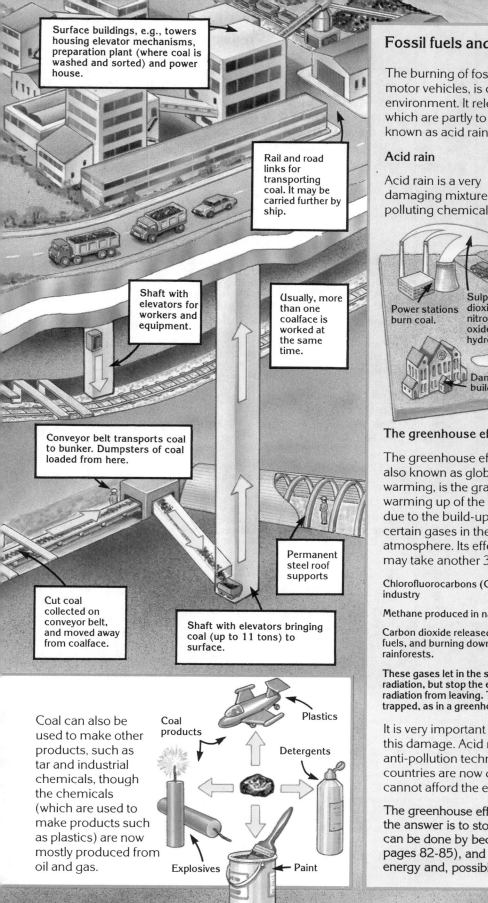

Surface buildings, e.g., towers housing elevator mechanisms, preparation plant (where coal is washed and sorted) and power house.

Rail and road links for transporting coal. It may be carried further by ship.

Shaft with elevators for workers and equipment.

Usually, more than one coalface is worked at the same time.

Conveyor belt transports coal to bunker. Dumpsters of coal loaded from here.

Permanent steel roof supports

Cut coal collected on conveyor belt, and moved away from coalface.

Shaft with elevators bringing coal (up to 11 tons) to surface.

Coal can also be used to make other products, such as tar and industrial chemicals, though the chemicals (which are used to make products such as plastics) are now mostly produced from oil and gas.

Coal products

Plastics

Detergents

Explosives

Paint

Fossil fuels and the environment

The burning of fossil fuels, in power stations and motor vehicles, is causing great damage to the environment. It releases gases into the atmosphere which are partly to blame for the two major problems known as acid rain and the greenhouse effect.

Acid rain

Acid rain is a very damaging mixture of polluting chemicals in rain and snow, produced as a result of burning fossil fuels.

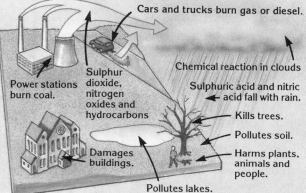

Cars and trucks burn gas or diesel.

Power stations burn coal.

Sulphur dioxide, nitrogen oxides and hydrocarbons

Chemical reaction in clouds

Sulphuric acid and nitric acid fall with rain.

Kills trees.

Pollutes soil.

Harms plants, animals and people.

Damages buildings.

Pollutes lakes.

The greenhouse effect

The greenhouse effect, also known as global warming, is the gradual warming up of the earth, due to the build-up of certain gases in the atmosphere. Its effects may take another 30 or more years to become obvious, but it may cause polar ice to melt, making the seas rise and flood low areas. It may also alter the world's climates, forcing major changes in farming patterns.

Chlorofluorocarbons (CFCs) produced by industry

Methane produced in nature.

Carbon dioxide released by burning fossil fuels, and burning down tropical rainforests.

These gases let in the sun's short-wave radiation, but stop the earth's long-wave radiation from leaving. This means heat is trapped, as in a greenhouse.

It is very important that we take action quickly to stop this damage. Acid rain can be prevented by using new anti-pollution technology in power stations. Many countries are now doing this, but others say they cannot afford the expensive devices needed.

The greenhouse effect is much harder to solve. Part of the answer is to stop burning so much fossil fuel. This can be done by becoming more energy-efficient (see pages 82-85), and by making more use of renewable energy and, possibly, nuclear power.

Oil and gas

Over 60% of the energy used in the world comes from oil and natural gas, so these substances have a vital role in the world's economy. Oil is the main fuel for transportation, and both oil and gas are burned to produce heat or used to produce other useful substances, such as plastics. The largest underground oil reserves are found in the Middle East. The largest gas reserves are in the former USSR.

How oil and gas were formed

Oil and gas were formed from the remains of plants and animals that once lived in the sea. Over millions of years, these remains were buried under mud and rock, under great pressure and at high temperatures. This gradually changed them into oil and gas.

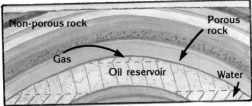

Non-porous rock
Porous rock
Gas
Oil reservoir
Water

Some oil and gas makes its way to the earth's surface and escapes.

Large amounts of oil and gas are trapped below ground in certain areas of rock, forming reservoirs.

Some reservoirs contain only gas.

An oil reservoir is a volume of rock which has spaces in it that are filled with oil. Rock with spaces in it, such as sandstone, is called porous rock. You can imagine a sandstone reservoir as a huge container of marbles, with oil in the spaces between them.

Recovering oil and gas

Geologists work out where there may be oil and gas by studying the rock structure. If oil is discovered, production wells are drilled to bring it up to the surface. Gas and water are then taken out, and it is pumped through pipelines to a refinery.

Large oil refinery

At the refinery, oil is broken down into many different forms (see main picture, right).

Oil is transported to and from refineries by pipeline or in large ships called oil tankers.

Oil rig in the North sea

The gas which is brought up is cleaned and treated. Firstly, water and other liquids are removed from it. It is then usually separated and used in various ways (see page 67). If it is to be transported, it may be turned into a liquid (by chilling).

As the oil fields on land are used up, more and more areas under the sea are being drilled for oil.

Rigs at sea have to survive the battering of powerful winds and waves.

About 20% of today's oil is produced from offshore platforms.

Refining and using oil

The crude oil (petroleum) that flows from a well is very thick. Before it can be used, it has to be cleaned and broken down into the different usable forms of oil, in a process called refining.

The different forms are separated in tall columns called fractionating columns. Each form of oil, called a fraction, is a mixture of hydrocarbons (substances made from just carbon and hydrogen). They range from "heavy" fractions (with large molecules) to "light" fractions.

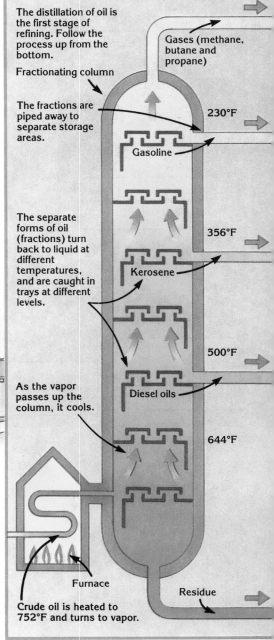

The distillation of oil is the first stage of refining. Follow the process up from the bottom.

Fractionating column

The fractions are piped away to separate storage areas.

The separate forms of oil (fractions) turn back to liquid at different temperatures, and are caught in trays at different levels.

As the vapor passes up the column, it cools.

Gases (methane, butane and propane)

230°F

Gasoline

356°F

Kerosene

500°F

Diesel oils

644°F

Furnace

Residue

Crude oil is heated to 752°F and turns to vapor.

Oil is a useful source of energy for several reasons. As a liquid, it can be stored and moved easily. It is easy to burn and has a high energy density (it has a lot of energy packed into a small volume). The different forms of oil are used in many different ways. The most important of these is transport.

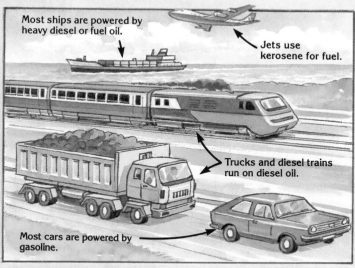

Most ships are powered by heavy diesel or fuel oil.

Jets use kerosene for fuel.

Trucks and diesel trains run on diesel oil.

Most cars are powered by gasoline.

Heavier oils are burned in the home for heat, and very heavy ones are used in power stations to produce electricity. Other forms of oil are converted into products like chemicals, plastics, and weedkillers.

Oil spills

Oil spills from tankers or oil rigs can cause a lot of damage to the environment. For example, the Exxon Valdez spill in Alaska, in March 1989, created an oil slick of around 960 square miles, causing damage that may take ten years or more to clear up. There are a number of techniques used to control this sort of damage. Try them yourself, on a smaller scale, by creating your own oil spill. Pour a small amount of vegetable cooking oil into a bowl, sink or tub of water.

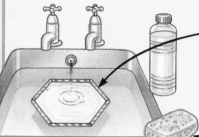

Try to work out the most effective way of controlling or breaking up the spill. Use drops of dishwashing liquid to break it up, or drinking straws connected with string, which make floating barriers to contain its spread.

Is it possible to mop up the spill using a sponge or paper towel?

Notice how oil sticks to your fingers. It kills seabirds by sticking their feathers together, so that they can no longer keep warm, fly or float.

The uses of gas

Natural gas is made up of a number of very light hydrocarbons, and is a clean fuel, containing no sulphur (one of the main causes of acid rain). After being cleaned and treated, it is usually separated into the different hydrocarbons.

The gas that is piped into the gas mains and delivered to houses and factories is made up almost entirely of methane, which is the hydrocarbon present in the largest amounts. The other hydrocarbons are used in other ways (see below).

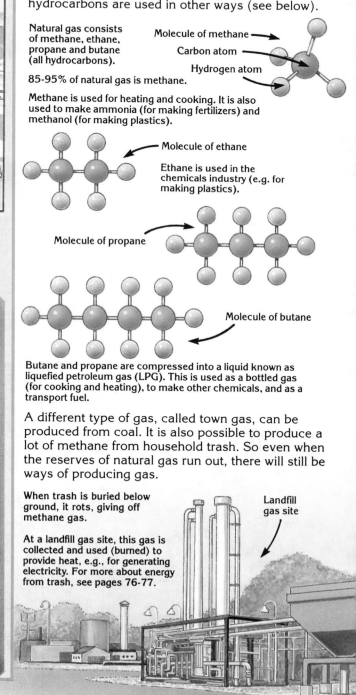

Natural gas consists of methane, ethane, propane and butane (all hydrocarbons).

85-95% of natural gas is methane.

Molecule of methane
Carbon atom
Hydrogen atom

Methane is used for heating and cooking. It is also used to make ammonia (for making fertilizers) and methanol (for making plastics).

Molecule of ethane

Ethane is used in the chemicals industry (e.g. for making plastics).

Molecule of propane

Molecule of butane

Butane and propane are compressed into a liquid known as liquefied petroleum gas (LPG). This is used as a bottled gas (for cooking and heating), to make other chemicals, and as a transport fuel.

A different type of gas, called town gas, can be produced from coal. It is also possible to produce a lot of methane from household trash. So even when the reserves of natural gas run out, there will still be ways of producing gas.

When trash is buried below ground, it rots, giving off methane gas.

At a landfill gas site, this gas is collected and used (burned) to provide heat, e.g., for generating electricity. For more about energy from trash, see pages 76-77.

Landfill gas site

Nuclear power

There are about 350 nuclear power stations around the world. They supply almost 20% of the world's electricity. Some of the countries that get an important part of their electricity from nuclear energy are the USA, the former USSR, Canada, France, Japan, the UK and Germany. Scientists once dreamed of a nuclear future with electricity that was "too cheap to meter," but nuclear power has not yet lived up to this, and there are many problems still to be overcome.

Types of nuclear reactor

There are several different types of nuclear reactor, all using nuclear fission (for more about this, see page 57). The most widely used is the pressurized water reactor (PWR), first built in the USA in 1957. The fast-breeder reactor (FBR) is a different sort of fission reactor that actually "breeds" its own fuel (it produces more fuel as a result of its nuclear reactions). But fast-breeders are proving very difficult to develop.

Scientists are also working on ways of controlling nuclear fusion (see page 57) with a view to developing fusion reactors. However, this research still has a very long way to go.

Inside a reactor

In a pressurized water reactor, heat is produced by nuclear fission in the core. The heat creates steam to drive the turbine generators that produce electricity (for more about this, see pages 70-71).

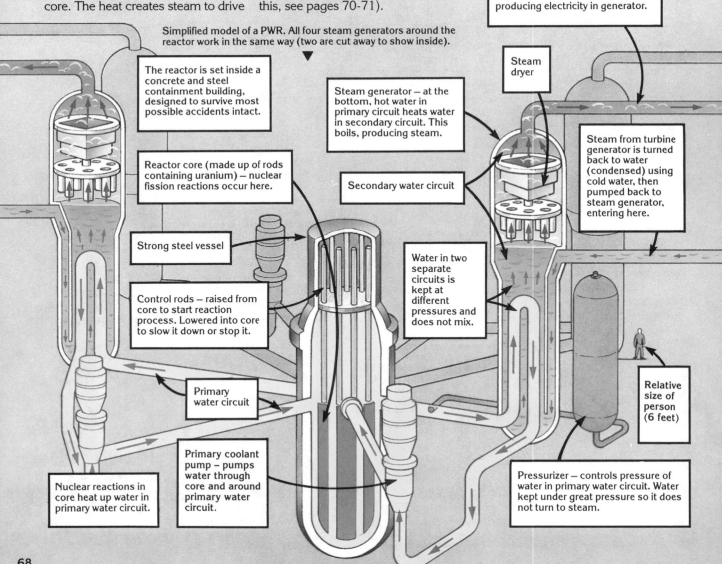

Simplified model of a PWR. All four steam generators around the reactor work in the same way (two are cut away to show inside).

Pipes take high pressure steam to turbine. Steam turns turbine shaft, producing electricity in generator.

The reactor is set inside a concrete and steel containment building, designed to survive most possible accidents intact.

Steam dryer

Steam generator — at the bottom, hot water in primary circuit heats water in secondary circuit. This boils, producing steam.

Steam from turbine generator is turned back to water (condensed) using cold water, then pumped back to steam generator, entering here.

Reactor core (made up of rods containing uranium) — nuclear fission reactions occur here.

Secondary water circuit

Strong steel vessel

Water in two separate circuits is kept at different pressures and does not mix.

Control rods — raised from core to start reaction process. Lowered into core to slow it down or stop it.

Relative size of person (6 feet)

Primary water circuit

Nuclear reactions in core heat up water in primary water circuit.

Primary coolant pump — pumps water through core and around primary water circuit.

Pressurizer — controls pressure of water in primary water circuit. Water kept under great pressure so it does not turn to steam.

Nuclear fuel

Uranium is the main nuclear fuel. It is mined in places throughout the world, such as North and South America, India, Africa, Australia and the former USSR.

Mined uranium is first purified, and then often "enriched" by adding more uranium atoms of one special type. This type is far more likely to undergo nuclear fission than the other type, which makes up most of the ore. The enriched uranium is made into pellets, which are put together to form rods (see page 68).

Two pellets of nuclear fuel for use in a PWR are equivalent to 2¾ tons of coal.

This is enough to produce all the electricity one person in the UK uses in a year.

Radioactivity

Some substances, like uranium and plutonium, are radioactive. This means they are unstable and give off particles or rays, known as radiation.

There are three main types of radiation – alpha, beta and gamma. Each has different characteristics, but all can cause damage, especially cancer, in humans. Neutron radiation is another kind of radiation, found in the core of nuclear reactors.

This sign warns of the presence of radioactive substances.

Nuclear power workers must wear or carry meters which show if they have been exposed to too much radiation.

Problems

Power stations using coal and oil are a major source of environmental problems such as acid rain and the greenhouse effect. Although nuclear power is a "cleaner" way of producing power in this sense, it also has its own set of problems. These must be solved before we increase our use of nuclear power.

Radioactive waste

The large amounts of radioactive waste created by the nuclear process cannot be destroyed. Some of it is so dangerous that it must be isolated for hundreds of thousands of years.

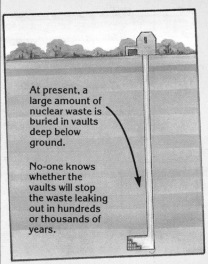

At present, a large amount of nuclear waste is buried in vaults deep below ground.

No-one knows whether the vaults will stop the waste leaking out in hundreds or thousands of years.

Cost

Nuclear power stations are relatively cheap to run, but expensive to build, and there are many hidden costs – such as the costs of research and dealing with nuclear waste.

Accidents

The consequences of a nuclear accident can be many times more serious than those of accidents that occur in other power industries. The nuclear accident in 1986 at Chernobyl, in the former USSR, showed this very clearly. It killed 30 people and exposed thousands more to radiation. It also contaminated millions of square miles of land.

The damage at Chernobyl could have been even worse if there had been a meltdown.

In a meltdown, the core melts due to the intense heat.

The radioactive material then burns through the containment building into the ground, through the rock, and into the underground water system.

Make up your own mind

You can get hold of a lot of information about nuclear power, and be able to compare the arguments for and against, by writing to electricity and nuclear energy organizations, and to anti-nuclear campaign groups. You could try organizing the arguments in a pamphlet or on a wall chart, and then hold a discussion at school or your local youth center.

The electricity industry

Electricity is very important to our modern way of living. It is hard to imagine life without it. Electricity is mostly produced in power stations, using large generators. These are usually powered by steam, which is produced by burning fossil fuels or from the heat of nuclear reactions. Some smaller generators, though, are driven by diesel engines, and others by water and wind power.

Generators

A generator is a machine which produces electricity from mechanical energy. The simplest type (for example, a bicycle dynamo) uses the mechanical energy (for example, of the moving bicycle) to turn a magnet inside a fixed coil of wire. Because of the relationship between magnetism and electricity, this produces electricity in the wire.

In a power station generator, the magnet used is a powerful electromagnet. It is turned inside a fixed coil of wire by a piece of machinery called a turbine which is turned by jets of steam. The whole generator produces very large amounts of electricity. The electromagnet itself is supplied with a current to make it work (see page 71).

Many out-of-the-way communities, not connected to a grid system (see page 71), depend on small generators for their electricity. These use diesel engines, instead of steam, to turn the turbine shaft. Places such as hospitals also have back-up diesel generators, in case something stops their supply of electricity from the grid system.

Energy from the sun, wind, waves, tides and flowing water can also be used to produce electricity. These are called renewable energy sources (see pages 73-81).

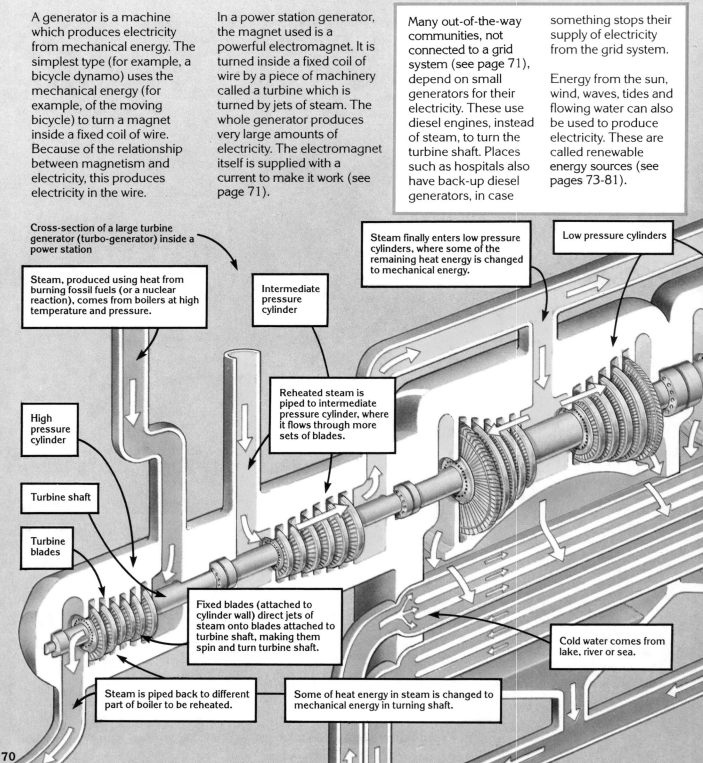

Cross-section of a large turbine generator (turbo-generator) inside a power station

Steam, produced using heat from burning fossil fuels (or a nuclear reaction), comes from boilers at high temperature and pressure.

Intermediate pressure cylinder

Steam finally enters low pressure cylinders, where some of the remaining heat energy is changed to mechanical energy.

Low pressure cylinders

High pressure cylinder

Reheated steam is piped to intermediate pressure cylinder, where it flows through more sets of blades.

Turbine shaft

Turbine blades

Fixed blades (attached to cylinder wall) direct jets of steam onto blades attached to turbine shaft, making them spin and turn turbine shaft.

Cold water comes from lake, river or sea.

Steam is piped back to different part of boiler to be reheated.

Some of heat energy in steam is changed to mechanical energy in turning shaft.

Electromagnets

An electromagnet is a magnet made by coiling a piece of wire around a piece of a certain type of material, such as iron. The magnet can be "switched on" (producing a magnetic field) by putting an electric current through the wire. On page 72, you can see how to make your own electromagnet.

Small electromagnets are used in electric bells.

When the switch is pressed (closed), the circuit is completed. The electromagnet is turned on and the metal arm is attracted.

The hammer strikes the bell.

The movement of the arm breaks the circuit, switching off the magnet (the arm goes back).

If the switch is still being pressed, the magnet goes on again (the process is repeated).

Metal arm

Circuit breaks here.

Hammer

Battery

Electric bell

Electromagnet

Switch

Turbine shaft rotates very rapidly (about 3,000 times a minute).

Generator

Turbine shaft is linked directly to electromagnet (rotor) which turns inside fixed coil of wire (stator), producing electricity.

Fixed coil

Electromagnet

Steam is condensed (turned to water) by passing it over pipes of cold water.

Condenser

Condensed steam (water) is pumped back to boiler, to be turned back into steam.

The grid system

Electricity produced in power stations is fed into a network of cables known as a grid. This links the power stations together and carries the electricity to where it is needed – places such as homes, offices and factories. Devices called transformers are used to increase the voltage of the electricity fed into the grid system, and decrease it at the other end (people's homes and places of work). The voltage is the measure of the force that drives the current through the wires. You can think of it as the amount of pressure "pushing" the electricity through the wires.

It is easier, and cheaper, to transmit electricity at high voltage, because less electricity is "lost" through heating the cables. However, it would not be safe to use very high

Electricity cables are usually suspended from pylons or buried underground, because they carry very dangerous high voltage electricity.

Transformers at power stations increase the voltage from 25,000V to 400,000V.

High voltage electricity cables are made of aluminium (a good conductor).

voltage in the home, so it has to be stepped down to a much lower level. Different countries use different household voltage levels (usually 110V or 240V).

Saving electricity

If electricity is used carefully and not wasted, then less will need to be produced. This means we will not have to use as much coal, oil or nuclear fuel, and the problems of acid rain, the greenhouse effect and nuclear waste will be reduced. On the right are some suggestions for saving electricity in the home.

Turn off lights when they are not in use.

Don't fill electric kettles with more water than you need. They can use a lot of electricity.

Avoid wasteful electrical appliances, like electric toothbrushes. You can brush your teeth better yourself.

Take showers instead of baths. They use less hot water.

For more about saving energy in the home, see page 82.

Making an electromagnet

Electromagnets are introduced on page 71. They are used in power station generators, but have many other uses, too, such as lifting old cars in scrap metal yards. Below you can find out how to make your own electromagnet and switch system.

What you will need

4.5 volt battery
5 ft and 20 in lengths of thin, single-core wire
6 in long iron or steel bolt (or nail)
Switch (paper clip, 2

thumbtacks and small block of wood or piece of stiff cardboard)
Paper clips or iron filings
tape

What to do

Strip 1 in of the insulating plastic coating from both ends of the two wires, using a pair of scissors or a pair of pliers.

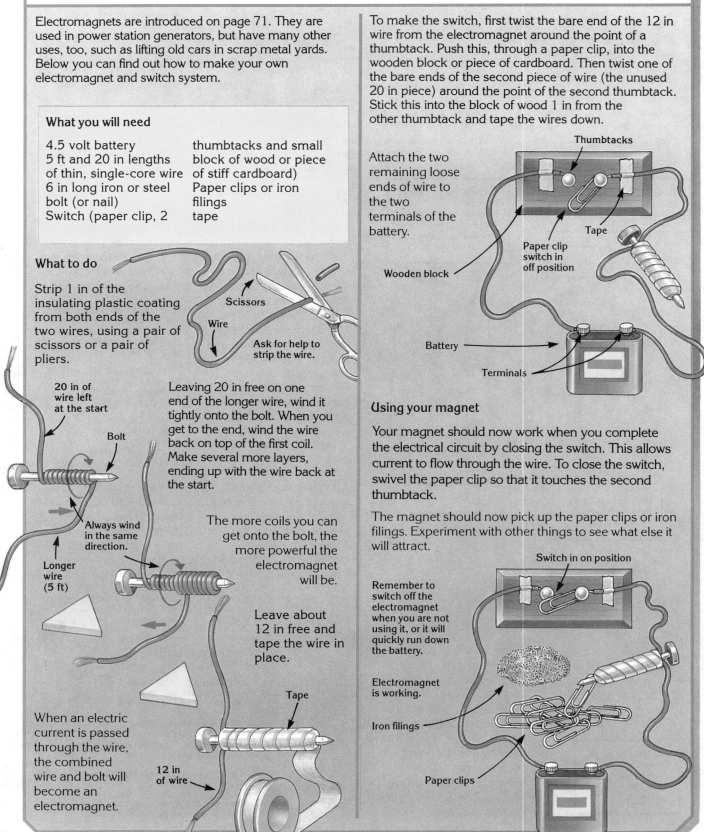

Scissors

Wire

Ask for help to strip the wire.

20 in of wire left at the start

Bolt

Always wind in the same direction.

Longer wire (5 ft)

Leaving 20 in free on one end of the longer wire, wind it tightly onto the bolt. When you get to the end, wind the wire back on top of the first coil. Make several more layers, ending up with the wire back at the start.

The more coils you can get onto the bolt, the more powerful the electromagnet will be.

Leave about 12 in free and tape the wire in place.

Tape

When an electric current is passed through the wire, the combined wire and bolt will become an electromagnet.

12 in of wire

To make the switch, first twist the bare end of the 12 in wire from the electromagnet around the point of a thumbtack. Push this, through a paper clip, into the wooden block or piece of cardboard. Then twist one of the bare ends of the second piece of wire (the unused 20 in piece) around the point of the second thumbtack. Stick this into the block of wood 1 in from the other thumbtack and tape the wires down.

Attach the two remaining loose ends of wire to the two terminals of the battery.

Thumbtacks

Tape

Paper clip switch in off position

Wooden block

Battery

Terminals

Using your magnet

Your magnet should now work when you complete the electrical circuit by closing the switch. This allows current to flow through the wire. To close the switch, swivel the paper clip so that it touches the second thumbtack.

The magnet should now pick up the paper clips or iron filings. Experiment with other things to see what else it will attract.

Switch in on position

Remember to switch off the electromagnet when you are not using it, or it will quickly run down the battery.

Electromagnet is working.

Iron filings

Paper clips

Renewable energy

Renewable energy sources (also known just as "renewables") are those that will not run out. They are constantly renewed in the cycles of the natural world (see pages 62-63) and are likely to play an increasingly important part in providing our energy in the future. The renewables include the sun, winds, waves, tides, rivers and plant matter. On the following pages (73-81), you can find out more about these different energy sources.

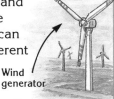

Solar cells

Wind generator

Renewable sources will be able to provide a great deal of energy, while causing far less damage to the environment than nuclear or fossil fuel sources. They do not produce as much waste or pollution, and do not contribute as much to major problems such as the greenhouse effect.

Tidal barrage

Dam

Solar energy

The sun provides the earth with enormous amounts of energy, some of which can be used for heating purposes and to produce electricity. This is known as solar energy, and is one of the main types of renewable energy. Some people believe that solar energy will be the main source of our energy in the long-term future.

Passive solar heating

The sun gives some heat to almost all buildings through their walls and windows. This is known as passive solar heating. The amount of solar energy used in this way can be increased by designing buildings with special features. The ancient Greeks were aware of this over 2,500 years ago.

The ancient Greeks used thick walls for their houses to absorb the sun's heat in the day, keeping the insides cool.

At night, heat stored in the walls kept the houses warm.

These basic ideas have been adapted and improved to increase the amount of useful energy supplied free by the sun. Modern houses, offices and other buildings designed with passive solar features need less heating, and save a lot of money in bills.

This house in Milton Keynes, England shows some passive solar features.

The house is positioned so that large windows on the south side make the most of the sunshine. They have long, heavy curtains to keep out the cold at night.

The house is well insulated (with the methods shown on page 82) to keep the warmth in.

Passive solar experiment

This experiment shows how the sun's heat can be used to heat the inside of a house, and how having a window facing the sun can increase the amount of heat captured. It shows the effects of passive solar heating.

Get two similar cardboard boxes and cut a large window in one. Cover this with plastic wrap, taping it down securely.

Paint each box white or cover them with white paper.

Place a thermometer through the top of each box. Make sure it has a cover (e.g. an upturned mug).

Place both boxes in the sun, making sure the window points towards the sun.

Record the temperatures every ten minutes, and make a graph of the results.

You should find that the box with the window becomes hotter more quickly.

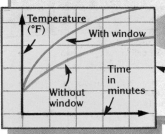

Temperature (°F)

With window

Without window

Time in minutes

Active solar heating

Active solar heating systems "collect" heat in one area, and then move this heat (using a device such as a pump or a fan) to another area. They are usually used to provide hot water, but can also be used to produce high temperatures for generating electricity.

Active solar heating is more effective in sunny countries. For example, in Israel it produces 90% of the hot water used in houses. The most common solar water heater is the flat plate collector (also called a solar panel).

This form of water heating was first used in the USA in the 1890s. Scientists have since improved on the basic design, by using special glass (to reflect less radiation), different surfaces (to absorb heat better) and vacuum tubes (to lessen heat loss).

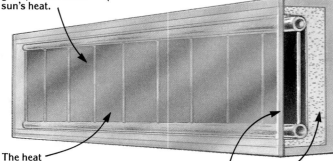

Flat plate collector

Blackened metal plate (behind the glass) absorbs the sun's heat.

The color black absorbs most of the sun's radiation, and so heats up quickly. White, however, reflects this radiation, and so keeps much cooler.

The heat from the plate is passed on to water running through pipes welded to the plate.

The glass cover and insulation material prevent the heat from escaping.

Making a solar water heater

It is easy to make a simple solar water heater. All you need is a long black hose. On a sunny day, coil this up so that as much of the hose as possible is in the sunshine (as shown below).

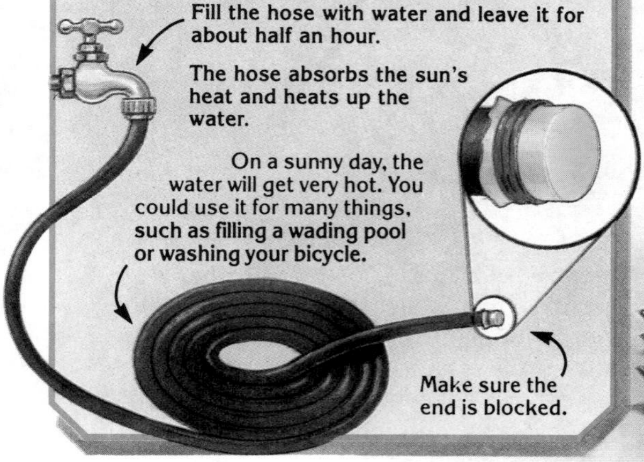

Fill the hose with water and leave it for about half an hour.

The hose absorbs the sun's heat and heats up the water.

On a sunny day, the water will get very hot. You could use it for many things, such as filling a wading pool or washing your bicycle.

Make sure the end is blocked.

Some solar collectors produce very high temperatures, which are used in industry and research, and for generating electricity. Temperatures of up to 5,400°F can be produced by combining flat mirrors and parabolic (curved) reflectors to concentrate and focus the sun's rays onto a very small area.

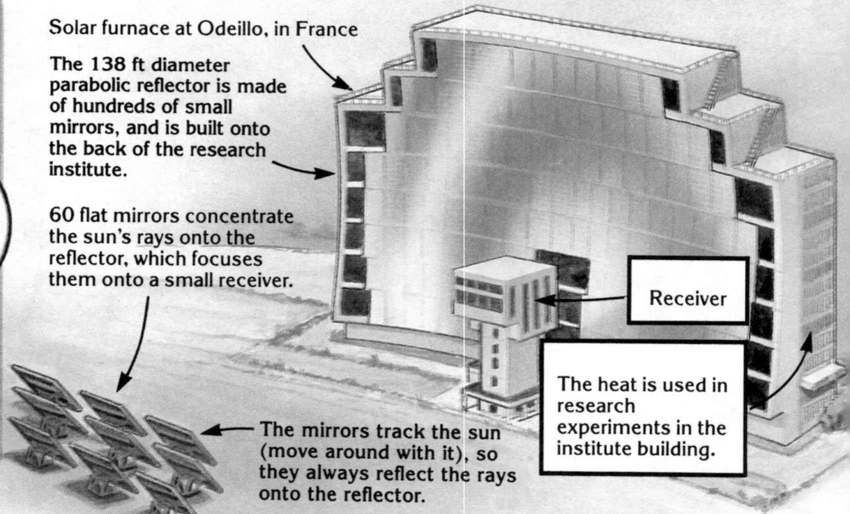

Solar furnace at Odeillo, in France

The 138 ft diameter parabolic reflector is made of hundreds of small mirrors, and is built onto the back of the research institute.

60 flat mirrors concentrate the sun's rays onto the reflector, which focuses them onto a small receiver.

The mirrors track the sun (move around with it), so they always reflect the rays onto the reflector.

Receiver

The heat is used in research experiments in the institute building.

Solar cells

A solar (or photovoltaic) cell turns the energy in sunlight directly into electricity. The most common type is made from silicon, the main ingredient of sand. Solar cells were first developed in the 1950s for use on satellites, but were extremely expensive to produce.

A lot of research into new materials and techniques has gone into the design of modern solar cells. They are now much cheaper and more efficient, and are beginning to be produced in much greater numbers. They are already used quite widely, and for a number of different purposes.

A solar powered calculator includes a solar cell.

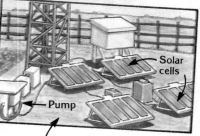

Solar cells powering a water pump in Mali, West Africa.

Solar cells can produce electricity even when the sun is behind clouds.

Solar cells

Pump

More solar projects

Below are two more projects which show how the sun's energy can be put to work.

Making a solar oven

The heat of the sun can be used in a simple solar oven to bake food. The instructions here describe how to make one of these ovens. After trying it out, you could also try to invent a larger oven, using the same idea, to bake larger pieces of food.

What you will need

2 Styrofoam cups
A large plastic container, such as a "family size" yogurt or salad bowl
Some newspaper
A sheet of black paper
A large sheet of paper or cardboard
Plastic food wrap
Aluminum foil
Some food (e.g. sliced carrot or apple)
Tape

What to do

Line one of the cups with black paper, and place the food inside it. Tightly cover the top with plastic wrap.

Plastic wrap

Black paper

Styrofoam cup

Food

The black paper absorbs the sun's heat and the plastic wrap prevents any hot air escaping.

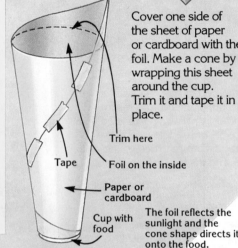

Cover one side of the sheet of paper or cardboard with the foil. Make a cone by wrapping this sheet around the cup. Trim it and tape it in place.

Trim here

Tape

Foil on the inside

Paper or cardboard

Cup with food

The foil reflects the sunlight and the cone shape directs it onto the food.

Place the cup and cone inside the other cup, and then place it all in the large pot, packing it with crumpled newspaper or tissue paper (this will insulate the solar oven).

Second cup

Large pot

Tissue paper

Place your solar oven in the sunshine, angled towards the sun, and leave it until the food is cooked. The time this takes will depend on how hot the sun is, but apple or carrot will take about half an hour in bright sunshine.

You may have to move the container as the sun moves.

Sunshine

Solar oven

Making a solar still

Solar stills are used in the sunnier parts of the world to get pure water from impure water. You can make a simple version at home, but you will need a very sunny day for it to work properly.

What you will need

Large plastic bowl
Smaller bowl (e.g. a soup bowl)
Plastic food wrap
Small weight (e.g. a heavy coin)
Tape

What to do

Pour 1 in of salty water into the large plastic bowl and place the small bowl in the center. Cover the top of the large bowl with plastic wrap, sealing it with tape around the sides. Put the weight in the center of the plastic wrap, so that it pulls it down in the center.

Place the still outside in the hot sunshine. The water should turn to vapor (evaporate), and then turn back to water (condense) as it cools on the underside of the plastic wrap. The pure water should run down the inside of the wrap, and then drip into the small bowl. To help it condense, you could pour a little cold water on the top (to keep it cool).

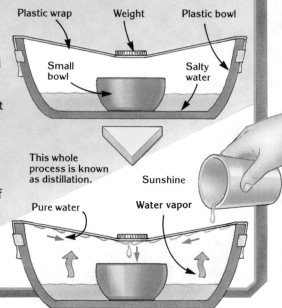

Plastic wrap   Weight   Plastic bowl

Small bowl

Salty water

This whole process is known as distillation.

Sunshine

Pure water   Water vapor

Energy from plants

Plants are the beginning of most of the energy chains on earth. They capture the sun's energy as they grow (see page 55), and animals eat them to create their own store of energy. Living or dead plant or animal matter (organic matter) is called biomass, and the energy it contains can be released and used in many different ways. It is all energy from plants, since the energy in usable animal matter, such as manure, comes indirectly from plants.

Biomass in poor nations

Over two billion people, almost half the world's population, depend on biomass to supply the energy they need for cooking, heating and light. Many of the poorer nations of Africa, Asia and South America get 80% or more of their energy from wood. Another important source of fuel for their fires and stoves is manure, which is burned when wood is scarce or too expensive.

Wood, manure or charcoal is burned on stoves and open fires that are very inefficient.

A typical three-stone fire, commonly used for cooking in Africa, Asia and South America.

Unfortunately, the burning of wood and manure creates serious problems. The demand for wood has resulted in deforestation. This is when so many trees are cut down that the soil erodes away and the climate begins to change. Manure would normally rot and return important chemicals to the soil, so when it is burned, less of these chemicals are returned to the soil, which means less food will grow.

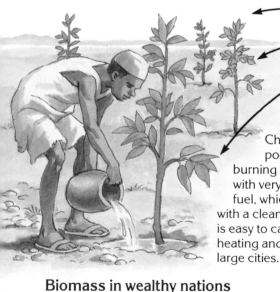

Tree-planting, or reforestation, is part of the solution to these problems.

Trees provide a source of energy, shade from the heat, and food for people and animals.

Trees also protect the soil by sheltering it from the wind and rain, and binding it together with their roots.

Charcoal is also widely used in poor countries. It is made by burning wood in a confined space (kiln) with very little oxygen. It is a very useful fuel, which burns at a high temperature with a clean flame and very little smoke. It is easy to carry and use, and is used for heating and cooking in homes in many large cities.

Biomass in wealthy nations

Some of the world's richer countries, like Canada, Sweden and Finland, have large forests and use a lot of wood to supply energy for homes and industries. In most of the other rich countries, though, wood is used mainly for building, and energy is supplied by other fuels. However, these countries are now beginning to recognize the potential in getting more of their energy from biomass.

Refuse

Household and commercial refuse (trash) is a major potential source of energy. A lot of it is actually biomass, like paper, food scraps and wood. It can be burned in special power stations, to produce heat and/or electricity. For example, 20% of the space and water heating in the Swedish city of Malmö comes from burning refuse.

A refuse-burning power station. Trucks deliver garbage, which is burned on a grate, producing hot gases. The heat from these boils water in a boiler, producing steam which is used to drive turbine generators (as in other power stations – see pages 70-71).

Crane

Boiler

Garbage truck

Refuse pit

Grate with burning refuse

Hot gases rise into boiler

Using old newspapers

Old newspapers can be collected for recycling. Find out if there is a recycling program in your area (contact your local environmental or conservation group). If not, you could turn your old newspapers into a useful fuel source. All you need are the newspapers and some thin wire.

Roll up the newspaper as tightly as you can, so it is about the same shape as a log of wood. Use the wire to tie it up securely. These newspaper logs can be burned in the same way as logs of wood.

Refuse can also be used to produce energy in other ways. When buried beneath the ground, it rots and produces gases. These gases have been a major nuisance, but they are now being used, particularly in the USA and parts of Europe. They are piped off and burned for heating or to generate electricity.

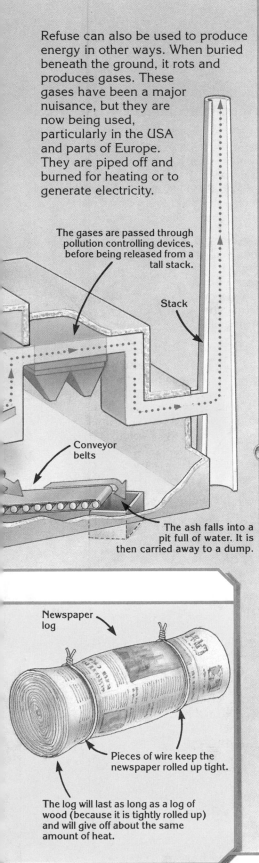

The gases are passed through pollution controlling devices, before being released from a tall stack.

Stack

Conveyor belts

The ash falls into a pit full of water. It is then carried away to a dump.

Newspaper log

Pieces of wire keep the newspaper rolled up tight.

The log will last as long as a log of wood (because it is tightly rolled up) and will give off about the same amount of heat.

Waste digesters

Sewage and waste from farms and industries are being used more and more to produce "biogas." The waste rots in containers called digesters, producing the gas. This can be burned to heat buildings and water.

This makes good use of the waste products, and reduces the pollution they would otherwise cause. Digesters are becoming more common, for example on large farms.

Waste digester on a farm

Slurry (semi-liquid waste) from the farm animals rots inside the large tank.

Gas (containing methane) is produced, stored and then burned to heat the farm buildings.

When the rotting has finished, the remains are spread on the fields as manure.

Straw and wood waste

Straw and wood waste, such as sawdust and wood chips, make excellent fuels. They can be burned for heating, or to dry crops.

Small straw-fired boiler

The burning straw heats up water, which is piped around the farm buildings.

Many farms, and some small country industries and estates, such as Woburn Abbey in England, are now using straw-fired furnaces to supply some of their energy for heating. The cost of setting up a system along these lines is soon made up in savings, as the source of this energy is freely available. The straw is burned in a furnace, which heats water in a boiler. This is then piped to where it is needed.

Enough heat is produced to keep several buildings warm.

Growing fuels

Some fast-growing plants (such as some types of tree) are now being grown on spare farmland, specifically to be cut down and used as a source of energy. These "forest farms" provide an extra source of income for the farmers. One way of raising trees for this purpose is called coppicing.

Certain plants are also being grown to produce different fuels for transportation. Sugar cane in Brazil is fermented to produce alcohol, which is used instead of gasoline. Other fuels that could be used to replace gas in the future are also being studied.

Traditional English coppice

The trees are cut off just above the ground and left to sprout.

The new shoots grow very fast because the tree already has a good root system.

The shoots are cut every 4-5 years for firewood and other uses.

Wind energy

The wind is one of the most promising of the renewable energy sources (see page 73). It can be used for a number of purposes, like producing electricity, or pumping water. Many countries are developing wind power technology, especially those whose geography means they get a lot of wind.

Uses of wind energy

The wind has been used for thousands of years to power sailing ships and windmills. Today it is beginning to be used more and more, and for a variety of purposes, some of which are described here. The greatest potential for using the wind is for the production of electricity.

The wind is used on farms to pump water up from under the ground. There are over a million water pumps in use, mainly in the USA, Canada and Australia.

Wind pump ▼

Wind vane – moves the blades to face the wind.

The wind makes the blades rotate. This makes the piston shaft move up and down inside the larger casing, pumping water from below the ground.

Blades

Water

Storage tank

Piston shaft

Water-bearing rock

A few modern ships are being fitted with sails (as well as engines) to harness the energy in the wind. This means they are able to save fuel. ▼

This Japanese cargo ship has two large metal and plastic sails.

A computer turns the sails so they are in the best position to catch the wind.

They can be folded up in very strong winds to protect them from damage.

Making a wind-measuring device

It is quite easy to make a simple device for measuring wind speeds. It will work best where there is a steady wind. You will need two protractors, a Ping-Pong ball, a flat piece of wood or plastic (such as a ruler), about 6 in of stiff thread, a needle, some sticky putty and some glue.

Thread the needle with the thread, and push it right through the Ping-Pong ball. Remove the needle and tie a knot in the thread so that the ball cannot come off. ▶

Thread

Needle

Ping-Pong ball

Sticky putty or glue

Hang the thread from the center of the straight edge of one protractor, so that the ball hangs just below the curved edge. Stick the thread on with a small piece of putty or some glue.

Marked sides of protractors

Now stick the other protractor to the first one with putty or glue, so that the thread is trapped inside. ▶

Glue the wood or plastic to the back to make a handle.

If you are left-handed, stick the handle on this side.

Hold the device level, and parallel to the wind (see below). When the ball is blown upwards, read off the angle that the thread reaches, and work out the wind speed from the table on the right.

Wind
0°
45°
90°

Angle (°)	Miles per hour
90	0
85	5-6.5
80	7-8.5
75	9-10
70	11-12
65	12.5-14
60	14.5-15
55	15.5-16
50	17-18
45	18.5-20
40	20.5-21.5
35	22-23.5
30	24-26
25	26.5-29
20	29.5-32.5

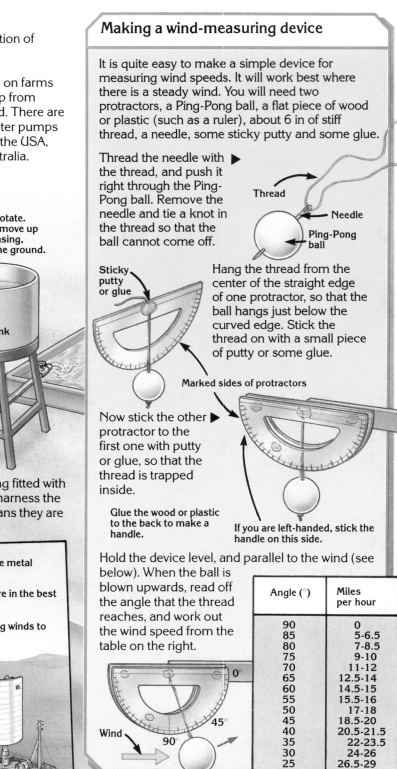

Electricity from the wind

The most important use of the wind is to produce electricity. This was first done in Denmark during the 1890s. Today, it is becoming more and more common.

Wind power has great potential for the future, as it is relatively safe and pollution-free. It can also generate electricity at the same price as fossil fuels and nuclear power.

To produce electricity, the wind is used to turn the shaft of a turbine, which is attached to a generator. This is a smaller version of a power station generator, which is driven by steam (see pages 70-71).

There are two main forms of wind turbine. One type has blades which are fixed on a vertical axis. This means it can catch the wind from any direction (see right).

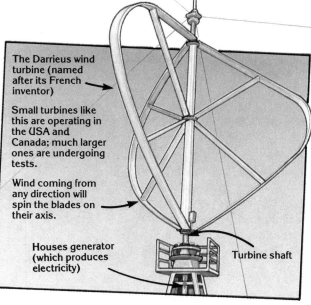

The Darrieus wind turbine (named after its French inventor)

Small turbines like this are operating in the USA and Canada; much larger ones are undergoing tests.

Wind coming from any direction will spin the blades on their axis.

Houses generator (which produces electricity)

Turbine shaft

Horizontal axis wind turbine

Lightning conductor

The turbine shaft (axis) is just about parallel to the ground.

Gears — these increase the speed of the shaft.

Blades

Hut can be turned, so that the blades always face into the wind.

Hut

Generator — driven by the rotating shaft. Produces electricity.

Tower

Most wind turbines now in use, though, are of the second type. They have horizontal axes (the shaft is parallel to the ground), which means they must be turned so that the blades face into the wind.

Most horizontal axis wind turbines have either two or three blades, and they differ greatly in size.

The best places to put wind turbines are where the wind is strongest and most consistent, such as on coasts and hilltops. However, this means they are very noticeable, and some people are opposed to them because of this. The machines also make a noise, so they cannot be placed close to houses.

The future of wind turbines

At the moment, there are over 20,000 wind turbines producing electricity around the world. Most of these are in the USA, Denmark and Holland. Many other countries, like Sweden, the UK, Spain, India and Australia, are developing wind power technology and are building their own wind turbines.

A "wind farm" (a collection of wind generators, producing a lot of electricity) at Altamont Pass, California.

There are three very large wind farms like this in California.

Scientists are now designing and testing bigger wind turbines. Most of those used at the moment are 80-100 ft high and generate several hundred kilowatts of power, but the new ones can be over 150 ft high and generate 3-4MW (a megawatt is a million watts). Their blades can be 200-300 ft in diameter.

There are plans to build large wind turbines out at sea, where the winds are stronger and steadier and where they would be less noticeable.

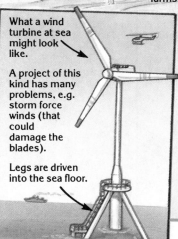

What a wind turbine at sea might look like.

A project of this kind has many problems, e.g. storm force winds (that could damage the blades).

Legs are driven into the sea floor.

Small wind turbines are important, too, especially for isolated farms and communities. Batteries are used to store the energy produced, for use when the wind is not blowing.

Over large areas, though, the wind is always blowing somewhere. By linking a lot of wind farms to the grid system, electricity can be sent from areas where the wind is blowing to areas where it is not, producing a more constant supply of electricity in all areas.

Energy from water

The energy in moving water is one of the most widely used of the renewable energy sources. It supplies over 20% of the world's electricity through the use of hydro-electric power stations. Other forms of water energy, especially tidal and wave energy, also have great potential, but more research still needs to be done to make the technology efficient and inexpensive.

Hydro-electric power

Hydro-electric power stations use the energy in moving river water to turn one or more turbines, producing electricity in generators (for more about turbine generators, see pages 70-71). Most rivers are capable of powering hydro-electric generators, but less than 10% of this potential is used in poor countries, and only about 30% in most richer ones. A few countries, though, such as Norway and Canada, already get a large part of their electricity from hydro-electric power stations.

Inside a hydro-electric power station

Each hydro-electric power station is specially designed for its site, as no two rivers are the same size or flow at the same speed. The amount of energy available to the turbines depends on two things – the distance (height) between the surface of the water and the turbines (called the head of water), and the rate that the water flows through the turbines.

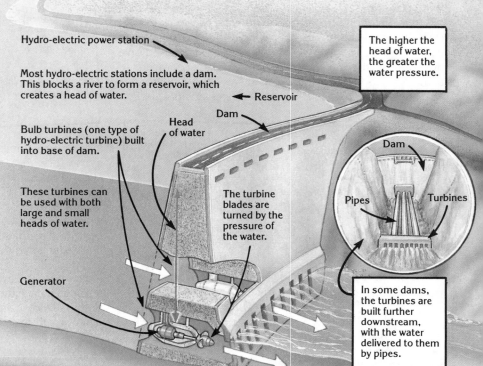

Hydro-electric power station

Most hydro-electric stations include a dam. This blocks a river to form a reservoir, which creates a head of water.

Bulb turbines (one type of hydro-electric turbine) built into base of dam.

These turbines can be used with both large and small heads of water.

Generator

Head of water

Reservoir

Dam

The turbine blades are turned by the pressure of the water.

The higher the head of water, the greater the water pressure.

Dam

Pipes

Turbines

In some dams, the turbines are built further downstream, with the water delivered to them by pipes.

Tidal energy

Turbines like those used in hydro-electric power stations can also produce electricity from the rising and falling of the tide. There are already a number of systems (called tidal barrages) in operation, and several others are being considered, including one across the estuary of the Severn River, in England.

The largest working tidal barrage is in the Rance estuary, in France. Built in 1966, it is 2,475 ft long and provides up to 240MW of power.

The Rance tidal barrage

There are 24 bulb turbines, with blades that can be reversed, so that electricity can be generated both when the tide is coming in and when it is going out.

The energy available depends on the size of the tidal basin and the tidal range (the difference in height between high and low tides).

Tidal barrages can cause environmental problems by disturbing an estuary's wildlife.

The bulb turbines are lined up along here.

Wave power

Some countries are looking at technology to harness the energy in the movement of ocean waves. This source of energy has huge potential. However, there are many problems to be tackled, such as dealing with high waves and strong winds in stormy weather.

An oscillating wave column, built near Bergen, in Norway (washed away in a storm in 1988)

Turbine blades, with shaft and generator above

Waves moved up inside the column, forcing the air above up through a turbine, generating electricity.

Problems with large dams

Building large hydro-electric dams can cause social and environmental problems.

Often a lot of land has to be cleared and flooded.

Many people may be forced to move from their homes.

Dams can become blocked by silt (soil carried by the river). In hot countries, they also bring an increase in diseases, like bilharzia, caused by tiny organisms in the still water.

Aerial view of dam and silted-up reservoir

Silt

Small dams are often a better choice than large ones, especially for supplying power to country areas. They cause less damage, and are easier to build. Almost 100,000 have been built in China since 1968 (providing over 5,000MW of power).

Making a water wheel

Water wheels have been used for centuries to use the energy in moving water to do work.

Below is an example of a simple model water wheel you can make with basic materials.

◀ Cut out two circles of cardboard, 8 in in diameter. Make a hole in the center of each.

Cut up two egg cartons to make 12 small buckets. Paint or varnish these to make the outsides waterproof.

Stick or staple the buckets to the cardboard making the water wheel.

Place a 6 in nail through the holes in the cardboard.

Tie some string very tightly to the nail and attach a weight (such as a pencil) to the end.

Buckets attached to cardboard circles

Open ends should face outwards.

◀ Use a piece of wood (such as a ruler) and some wire to support the nail.

Put the wheel under a tap and watch it lift the weight.

To attach the wire, make loops at both ends.

Experiment with different water speeds from the tap.

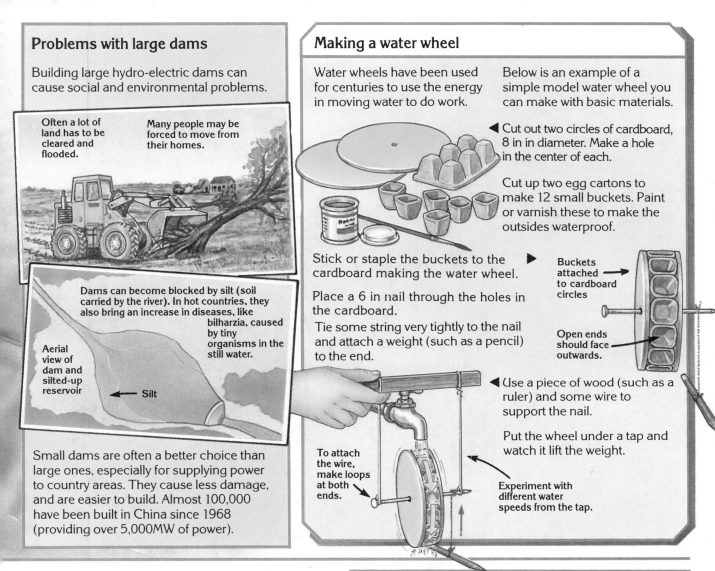

OTEC

In hot, equatorial areas there is another potential means of gaining energy from the oceans, by using the temperature difference between the layers of water. The method, still being researched at present, is called Ocean Thermal Energy Conversion (OTEC).

OTEC devices use warm surface water to heat up and vaporize a fluid with a low boiling point, such as ammonia. The moving vapor drives a turbine, generating electricity. Cold water from deeper down is then used to cool the vapor and condense it back to ammonia for recirculating.

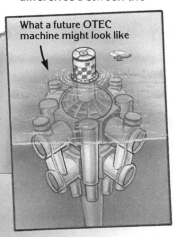

What a future OTEC machine might look like

Geothermal energy

Heat which comes from the earth itself is called geothermal energy. It is already used in some parts of the world, such as Iceland, where natural steam is produced as water passes over hot rock under the earth's surface. This steam is used to generate electricity.

Elsewhere, such as in France, warm water is pumped up from underground to heat blocks of apartments.

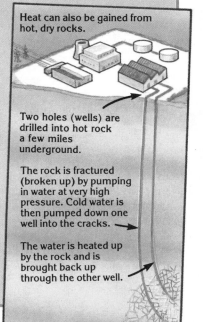

Heat can also be gained from hot, dry rocks.

Two holes (wells) are drilled into hot rock a few miles underground.

The rock is fractured (broken up) by pumping in water at very high pressure. Cold water is then pumped down one well into the cracks.

The water is heated up by the rock and is brought back up through the other well.

Energy efficiency

Being energy-efficient means continuing to do most of the things we do today, but using less energy to do them. If we save energy, less is needed, and we reduce the damage to the environment caused by producing energy. Being energy-efficient is the cheapest and simplest way to start solving serious environmental problems. On the next four pages, you can find out about saving energy.

You may not be in a position yourself to make many of the changes suggested, but if you know about them you can make other people aware of them.

Saving energy in the home

Many buildings, especially old ones, are very inefficient to heat, because they lose so much heat to the outside environment. By introducing a number of simple energy saving (conservation) measures, the cost of heating these buildings can often be cut by a half.

This shows where heat is lost from a house in winter, and how this heat loss can be reduced.

If you turn your heating down by a few degrees, you can save a lot of energy, and you probably won't notice the difference.

Insulating your hot water tank will make it heat up more quickly and stay hot for longer.

There are some more energy-saving ideas on page 71.

These energy-saving measures can also be used in larger buildings, such as schools and offices. Here, the amount of energy and money that can be saved is quite large. Find out if your school or community center can put some of these measures into action. You could do your part to help.

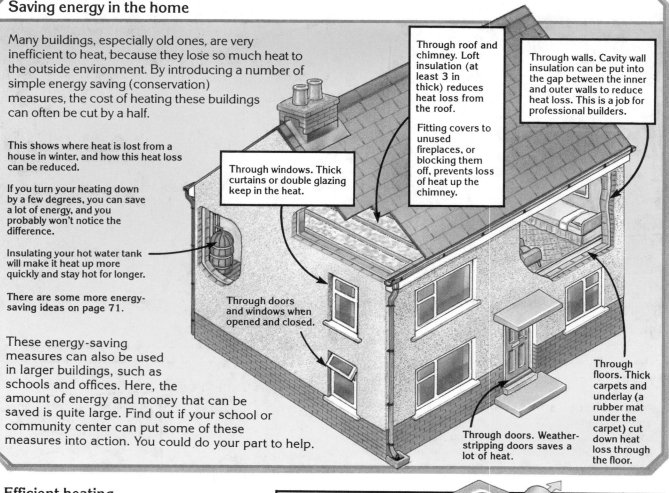

Through roof and chimney. Loft insulation (at least 3 in thick) reduces heat loss from the roof.

Fitting covers to unused fireplaces, or blocking them off, prevents loss of heat up the chimney.

Through walls. Cavity wall insulation can be put into the gap between the inner and outer walls to reduce heat loss. This is a job for professional builders.

Through windows. Thick curtains or double glazing keep in the heat.

Through doors and windows when opened and closed.

Through doors. Weather-stripping doors saves a lot of heat.

Through floors. Thick carpets and underlay (a rubber mat under the carpet) cut down heat loss through the floor.

Efficient heating

As well as preventing heat loss, it is important to make sure that the type of heating you use is as efficient as possible. There have been many developments in heating efficiency over the years, which have saved a great deal of energy and money for the people who have used them. Much more could still be done, though. The efficiency of a heating system varies according to the type of fuel it uses, whether it is in good or bad condition, and how sensibly it is used.

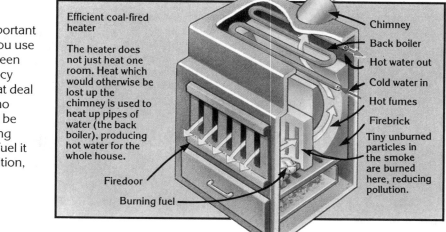

Efficient coal-fired heater

The heater does not just heat one room. Heat which would otherwise be lost up the chimney is used to heat up pipes of water (the back boiler), producing hot water for the whole house.

Chimney
Back boiler
Hot water out
Cold water in
Hot fumes
Firebrick
Tiny unburned particles in the smoke are burned here, reducing pollution.

Firedoor
Burning fuel

Supplying energy to homes

One of the most efficient ways to provide heating in towns and cities where buildings are close together is known as district, or community, heating. Instead of each house and office burning fuel to provide its own heating, the heat for all the buildings is produced at a central point (such as a boiler or a power station).

Power stations that produce both electricity and district heating are called combined heat and power (CHP) stations. For more about CHP, see page 84.

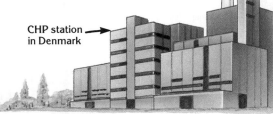

CHP station in Denmark

Household appliances

There are big differences in the energy efficiency of different makes of electrical appliances (such as fridges, stoves and irons). Your family can save a lot of electricity and money by using the ones that are the most energy efficient. Ask about the energy efficiency of different models when you are in the store to make sure your parents buy the most efficient.

Some refrigerators now on sale use only a fifth of the electricity used by other refrigerators of the same size, and some now being developed will use just a tenth.

If everyone in the UK who bought a refrigerator in the next 15 years bought the most efficient type, the total saving would be 1,800/MW (the power of 2 nuclear reactors).

Slow cookers

A very energy-efficient way of cooking is to use a slow cooker – a large, well-insulated casserole dish that plugs in and cooks food for 6-8 hours, using very little energy. Slow cooking itself is a very old cooking method, and is an excellent way to cook casseroles and soups. You can make an old-style slow cooker (a haybox cooker) very easily.

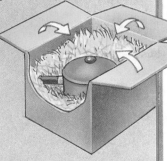

How to make and use a haybox cooker

Get a cardboard box that is large enough to fit a saucepan inside, with space around it.

Fill the box tightly with dry hay or straw, leaving a hole big enough for the saucepan.

Put the ingredients in the saucepan, put the lid on, and boil for 10 minutes (it is important to get the food very hot to start with). Then put the pan into the hole in the haybox, and cover it with another tightly-packed layer of hay or straw.

Close the flaps on the top of the box, and seal them with tape.

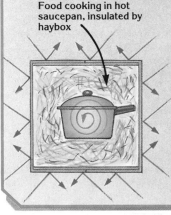

Food cooking in hot saucepan, insulated by haybox

Leave your food to cook for 6-8 hours. A meal put in the box in the morning will be cooked by the evening, and will only need to be reheated.

The hay acts as an insulating layer, keeping the heat in and the cold out.

You could try other insulating materials, such as crumpled-up newspaper or Styrofoam.

Energy efficient stoves

Many people in poor countries are not able to afford modern cooking and heating appliances, or the fuel that they burn. Many still burn wood on open fires and stoves, but, as more and more trees are cut down for fuel, whole areas are becoming deforested (losing all their trees).

This situation would improve if the open fires were replaced by low-cost, energy-efficient ones, but care must be taken not to disrupt the people's way of life. Open stoves not only give them heat, but also lighting at night. They are also important as the center of family life.

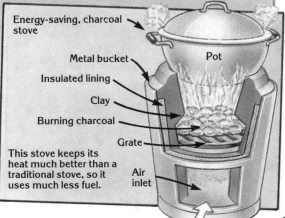

Energy-saving, charcoal stove

Metal bucket

Insulated lining

Clay

Burning charcoal

Grate

Pot

This stove keeps its heat much better than a traditional stove, so it uses much less fuel.

Air inlet

Efficiency in industry

Many of the basic energy-saving measures used in the home can also be used in buildings where people work. The buildings and machinery used in industry, however, are much larger and more complex, so there are also different problems to be faced in order to improve energy efficiency. There are a number of ways to solve these problems, and these need to be used more widely.

The heat wheel

The heat wheel is an energy-saving device used in industry. It uses the heat from warm air or hot fumes leaving a building or factory to warm up fresh, incoming air. A heat wheel recovers up to 80% of the heat in the outgoing air, saving a lot of energy.

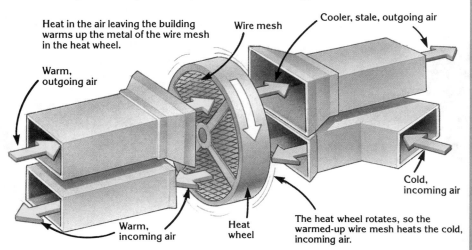

Heat in the air leaving the building warms up the metal of the wire mesh in the heat wheel.

Wire mesh

Cooler, stale, outgoing air

Warm, outgoing air

Cold, incoming air

Warm, incoming air

Heat wheel

The heat wheel rotates, so the warmed-up wire mesh heats the cold, incoming air.

People in industry and business should be encouraged to introduce energy-saving devices and techniques to old buildings, or add them to new ones as they are built. They may be expensive to buy, but they can save money, as well as energy, in the long term.

Embedded energy

In many industries, a lot of energy is used to make materials and goods – for example, to heat the furnaces in which steel and glass are made. This energy is sometimes known as embedded energy. If the materials, and the things which are made from them, are repaired, recycled and used again, then less energy needs to be used up in producing more materials and goods.

Any substance that is made using a lot of energy, such as steel or glass, has a lot of embedded energy.

Car

Glass windshield and windows

Steel body

Any object that is made from these substances, such as a car, also has a lot of embedded energy.

Combined heat and power

One important place to improve efficiency is in large power stations which use coal or oil. Only about 35% of the energy put in as fuel is converted into electricity. The rest is lost as heat. In the UK, for example, the heat lost from power stations is enough to heat every home in the country.

Combined heat and power (CHP) stations produce electricity and useful heat at the same time. Instead of being released, hot water from the production of electricity is piped to local buildings and used for space and water heating. This is known as district heating.

CHP stations produce slightly less electricity than ordinary power stations. But they use more of the heat produced, and can be twice as efficient overall (70-80% efficient).

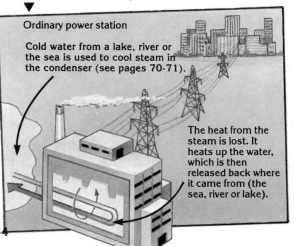

Ordinary power station

Cold water from a lake, river or the sea is used to cool steam in the condenser (see pages 70-71).

The heat from the steam is lost. It heats up the water, which is then released back where it came from (the sea, river or lake).

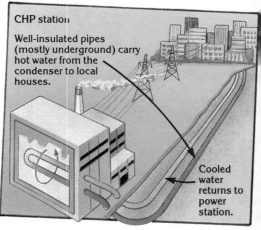

CHP station

Well-insulated pipes (mostly underground) carry hot water from the condenser to local houses.

Cooled water returns to power station.

There are also much smaller CHP generators which produce both electricity and heat in the same way as the larger ones. These can be used in all kinds of industrial buildings.

Efficiency in transportation

About a quarter of all the energy used in some industrialized nations is used in transportation. However, many means of transportation are very inefficient, both as machines and as ways of carrying people and goods. By using new technology, we could produce machines that are more energy-efficient. Also, by changing our ideas about the way we use transportation, we could create better, more energy-efficient transportation systems and a more pleasant, less polluted environment.

More efficient cars

Most cars are inefficient in the way they use energy. In the average car engine, only about 15% of the chemical energy stored in gasoline is actually converted into the movement energy of the car. The rest is lost as heat. Engineers are now working on new, more efficient cars and engines for the future.

A more energy-efficient car of the future ▶

Streamlined car body means there is less friction between the air and the car. The air flows more smoothly over the body, so less energy has to be used up in moving against it.

Lighter bodywork (perhaps made of strong, hard plastic) means the engine has to do less work (it has to move less weight) and so uses up less energy.

Smaller, more efficient engine (converts more of the chemical energy in gasoline into movement energy).

Cars and public transportation

Although cars can be very useful, even energy-saving cars can be an inefficient means of transportation. This is especially true in crowded areas, such as towns and cities. A car takes up road space and uses up a lot of energy, often to carry just one person.

As more cars are bought, traffic jams threaten to bring many large cities to a standstill.

Some cities, like San Francisco, are now introducing laws to reduce the number of private cars allowed on the streets.

Public transportation is a much more energy-efficient way to move people around. Many people would like to see private cars banned from city centers, and re-placed by much better public transportation systems, with cheap, regular and extensive services. This would also reduce pollution from exhausts.

The number of heavy trucks on the roads could also be reduced by introducing better rail systems. Trains are more energy efficient for moving people and goods over long distances.

Riding a bicycle

The bicycle is a very efficient machine. It takes little energy to travel comfortably over quite long distances. More people are now using bicycles, both for enjoyment and to keep fit. By not using gas, they help to save energy and reduce air pollution. Below are some ideas to help make a bicycle work more efficiently.

Keep the tires well pumped up. A flat tire has more surface touching the road. This causes friction and slows you down.

Keep the moving parts well oiled. Oil reduces friction, making it easier to ride.

Oil at the points labeled below.

Make sure the bicycle is the right size for you and the seat is at the correct height. If not, it will be harder to cycle (your leg muscles will not be working as efficiently as they could).

Handle-bars

Brakes

Wheels

Chain

Pedals

Energy in the future

Within the next few decades, there will have to be great changes in the way energy is used throughout the world. The way we produce and use energy at the moment is causing serious damage to the environment. At the same time, demand for energy is increasing as the world's population continues to grow, but there are only limited reserves of fossil fuels, which today provide about 80% of the world's energy. It is very important that everyone begins to use energy carefully and responsibly.

The growth of pollution

When coal was first burned in large quantities, during the Industrial Revolution in Europe in the 1800s, the pollution produced was mostly local. Towns and cities became very dirty and unhealthy.

Smog was a result of smoke from coal fires and factories mixing with fog.

Smog (a mixture of smoke and fog) in a large city in the 1870s.

Many people used to die from bronchitis and asthma when the smog was particularly bad.

Later, steps were taken to get rid of smog. Smokeless fuels were introduced and tall smoke stacks were built at power stations and factories to carry smoke away from local areas. But this meant that pollution was spread much further afield. For example, trees and lakes in Norway have been damaged by pollution from British power stations.

Tall smoke stacks release pollution high above the ground, where strong winds carry it away. often for hundreds of miles.

Norway

Prevailing winds

Acid rain damages trees and lakes.

Britain

As they grew wealthier, the industrialized countries burned larger amounts of fossil fuels. This has resulted in a gradual buildup of carbon dioxide in the atmosphere, which is one of the main causes of the greenhouse effect. This is a serious threat to the world's environment, and pollution has now become an international problem.

Energy use in rich countries

In most rich countries, people's lifestyles are very wasteful of energy. This is because modern lifestyles developed when energy was cheap and plentiful, and few people realized the dangers of pollution. But we now know about these dangers, and can see that some of our energy resources will soon become more scarce. Because of these things, we must begin to change the way we use energy.

Some people believe that more and more energy must be used to improve living standards. However, this is only true in countries which are still building up their industries. In nations with a lot of modern industries, there is a much less direct link between energy use and living standards.

In the USA, the large, "gas-guzzling" car used to be very common. Today, far more Americans drive smaller, more energy-efficient cars.

In Japan, the standard of living has continued to improve without an increase in energy use.

Japan used the same amount of energy in 1984 as it did in 1979, but there was a 23% increase in the country's wealth.

A lot of energy is saved by recycling materials and increasing energy efficiency.

An energy-efficient high-speed train in Japan

Energy use in poor countries

Many of the world's poorest countries have very large, growing populations, but their use of energy sources per person is low compared to the rich countries.

However, a number of these countries have plenty of coal and want to develop their industries in the same way as the rich countries have, to improve the standard of living of their people. This would mean a vast increase in energy use and world pollution, and would greatly speed up the rate at which world resources are used up.

In 1988:

One person in China used 0.73 tons of oil or equivalent*.

One person in North America used 8.86 tons of oil or equivalent.

One person in the Middle East used 3.05 tons of oil or equivalent.

For more about world resources and energy consumption, see pages 88-91. See page 90 for more of these "per head" figures.

Changes in energy use

Every few years something dramatic happens that changes the way people think about energy. These events affect the choices governments make about how to use energy in the future. For example, in 1973, the main oil-producing nations quadrupled the price of oil and threatened to stop supplying it to some countries. Then, in 1985, prices collapsed due to over-production. Another example is the nuclear accident at Chernobyl in the former USSR in 1986, which changed many people's minds about the safety of nuclear power.

Scientific discoveries are also unpredictable. For example, newly-developed substances called high temperature superconductors, which conduct electricity very efficiently, are likely to improve greatly the efficiency of machines and cables. Events like these will continue to happen, making long-term planning very difficult.

If oil prices are low, the car industry booms, and governments may build more oil-fired power stations.

If oil prices are high, governments may build more nuclear power stations, but fear of another accident like Chernobyl may mean a lot of public opposition.

A new, increasing awareness of environmental problems such as acid rain may mean governments take action to reduce pollution.

Solutions to the energy question

We are surrounded by sources of energy that can be used to make our lives more comfortable and enjoyable. But all energy sources have a cost, in terms of money and environmental damage. If they are used sensibly, we can continue to have enough energy without destroying our environment. To achieve this, we will have to make some changes, such as those suggested here.

The wealthy ▶ countries must reduce their energy use, perhaps by 50% by the year 2020, by being more energy-efficient.

◀ They must also share their knowledge and technology with the poor countries, to help them develop their own efficient and appropriate ways of producing energy.

Laws must be passed, and help given, to make sure anti-pollution technology is introduced and used in all countries.

There must be more ▶ cooperation to tackle world problems such as the greenhouse effect.

◀ There must be more research into renewable sources of energy, and a gradual switch away from fossil fuels to these cleaner, safer sources.

Solutions must be found to the problems of nuclear waste and the safety of nuclear reactors, before there is a further increase in the use of nuclear power around the world.

---

*See pages 88 and 89 for an explanation of "oil equivalent."

World energy facts

On the next four pages there are some charts, maps and graphs which give an idea of the different amounts of energy produced and consumed in different areas of the world, and also the estimated reserves of these sources around the world.

Production and consumption of fossil fuels

The charts below give the amounts of oil, natural gas and coal produced (brought out of the ground to be used or sold) and consumed (used) by different areas of the world in 1988.

Each area is a group of countries (the standard groups used in such statistics in 1988, before all the changes in the late 1980's and early 1990's). If the figure for a particular country within a group is significantly larger than the figures of the other countries in that group, it is given separately.

Key to country groups

- North America (USA and Canada)
- Latin America (except Cuba, a socialist country)
- Western Europe
- Middle East
- Africa
- Asia (except socialist countries)
- Australia and New Zealand
- Socialist countries*

Oil production, 1988 (million tons)

600.5 (USA 508.7)
375.1 (Mexico 155.1)
217.8 (UK 125.6)
813.2 (Saudi Arabia 282.8)
288.7
148.6
30.5
859.4 (USSR 686.4)

World total: 3333.9

Oil consumption, 1988 (million tons)

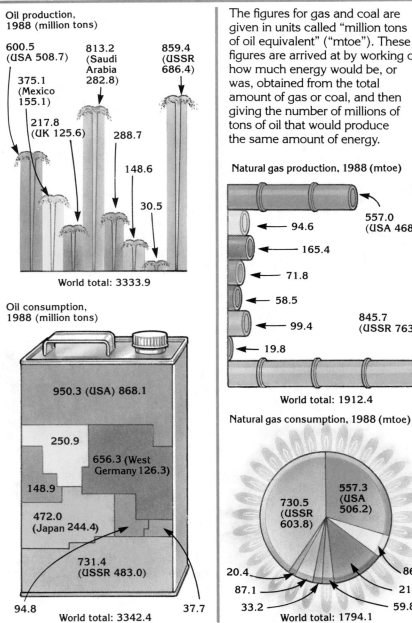

950.3 (USA) 868.1
250.9
656.3 (West Germany 126.3)
148.9
472.0 (Japan 244.4)
731.4 (USSR 483.0)
94.8
37.7

World total: 3342.4

The figures for gas and coal are given in units called "million tons of oil equivalent" ("mtoe"). These figures are arrived at by working out how much energy would be, or was, obtained from the total amount of gas or coal, and then giving the number of millions of tons of oil that would produce the same amount of energy.

Natural gas production, 1988 (mtoe)

557.0 (USA 468.3)
94.6
165.4
71.8
58.5
99.4
19.8
845.7 (USSR 763.1)

World total: 1912.4

Natural gas consumption, 1988 (mtoe)

730.5 (USSR 603.8)
557.3 (USA 506.2)
20.4
87.1
33.2
86.9
218.9
59.8

World total: 1794.1

Coal production, 1988 (mtoe)

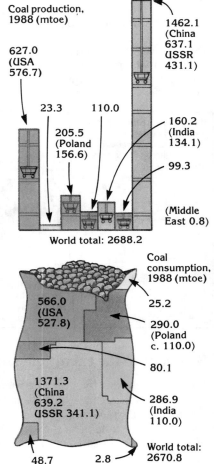

627.0 (USA 576.7)
23.3
205.5 (Poland 156.6)
110.0
1462.1 (China 637.1 USSR 431.1)
160.2 (India 134.1)
99.3
(Middle East 0.8)

World total: 2688.2

Coal consumption, 1988 (mtoe)

566.0 (USA 527.8)
1371.3 (China 639.2 USSR 341.1)
25.2
290.0 (Poland c. 110.0)
80.1
286.9 (India 110.0)
48.7
2.8

World total: 2670.8

Some interesting points can be made from looking at figures such as these. For instance, countries such as the USA consume far more oil than they produce. These countries must rely on buying oil from other countries. Also, you can see that the top five coal producers (the countries named) are also the top five consumers.

* Albania, Bulgaria, China, Cuba, Czechoslovakia, East Germany, Hungary, Kampuchea, Laos, Mongolia, North Korea, Poland, Romania, USSR, Vietnam, Yugoslavia.

Nuclear and hydro-electric energy

Most of the world's energy comes from burning fossil fuels. But some energy is also produced by nuclear power stations and the various renewable sources. A complete picture of energy consumption is not possible without figures for these sources, but unfortunately some figures are incomplete and unreliable, in particular those for the burning of wood in Third World countries (in many cases, the main source of energy in these countries). The only clear international figures available for non-fossil sources are for electricity obtained from nuclear and hydro-electric power. As before, mtoe units are used, in this case being the amount of oil which would fuel an oil-fired power station to produce the same amount of electricity.

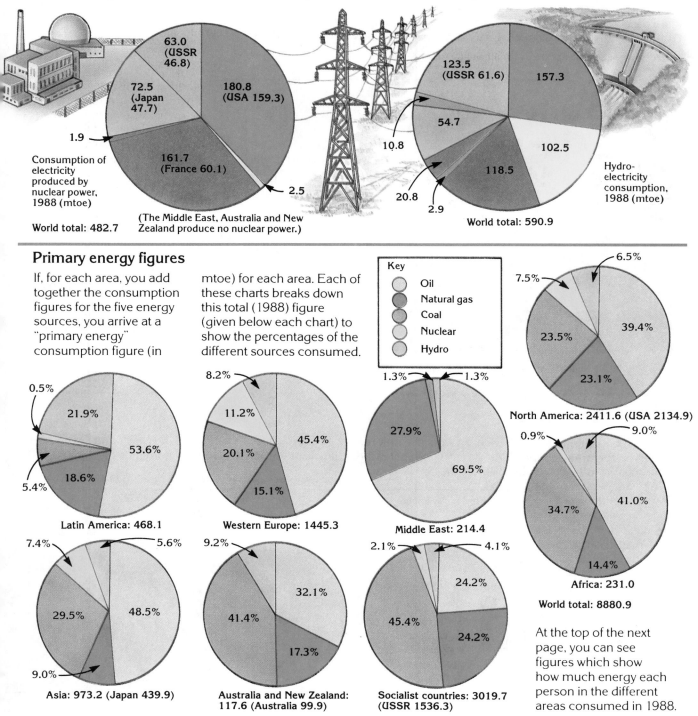

63.0 (USSR 46.8)
180.8 (USA 159.3)
72.5 (Japan 47.7)
1.9
161.7 (France 60.1)
2.5

Consumption of electricity produced by nuclear power, 1988 (mtoe)

(The Middle East, Australia and New Zealand produce no nuclear power.)

World total: 482.7

123.5 (USSR 61.6)
157.3
54.7
10.8
102.5
118.5
20.8
2.9

Hydro-electricity consumption, 1988 (mtoe)

World total: 590.9

Primary energy figures

If, for each area, you add together the consumption figures for the five energy sources, you arrive at a "primary energy" consumption figure (in mtoe) for each area. Each of these charts breaks down this total (1988) figure (given below each chart) to show the percentages of the different sources consumed.

Key
- Oil
- Natural gas
- Coal
- Nuclear
- Hydro

0.5%
21.9%
53.6%
5.4%
18.6%

Latin America: 468.1

8.2%
11.2%
45.4%
20.1%
15.1%

Western Europe: 1445.3

1.3% / 1.3%
27.9%
69.5%

Middle East: 214.4

6.5%
7.5%
39.4%
23.5%
23.1%

North America: 2411.6 (USA 2134.9)

0.9% / 9.0%
41.0%
34.7%
14.4%

Africa: 231.0

World total: 8880.9

7.4% / 5.6%
48.5%
29.5%
9.0%

Asia: 973.2 (Japan 439.9)

9.2%
32.1%
41.4%
17.3%

Australia and New Zealand: 117.6 (Australia 99.9)

2.1% / 4.1%
24.2%
45.4%
24.2%

Socialist countries: 3019.7 (USSR 1536.3)

At the top of the next page, you can see figures which show how much energy each person in the different areas consumed in 1988.

Energy use and population

This graph looks at the 1988 primary energy consumption figures, shown on page 89, in terms of how much energy (on average) was used per person in each of the areas. The figures are worked out by dividing the total primary energy consumption of each area by its population.

It must be remembered that the primary energy figures are based on the five "major" energy sources, and that other sources of energy, such as wood, animal waste and refuse, and also solar, wind and wave power, are not taken into account.

The area groups are the same as on pages 88-89 (for example, "Asia" still means non-communist Asia), but some countries have been separated out. You can see that there are some very large differences between the rich and poor areas of the world. One person in North America, for example, used over 23½ times more energy than a person in Africa.

Tons of oil or equivalent (see pages 88 and 89) used per head in 1988

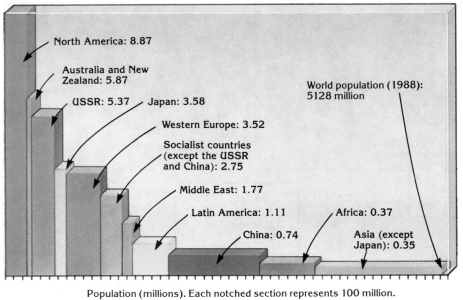

North America: 8.87
Australia and New Zealand: 5.87
USSR: 5.37   Japan: 3.58
Western Europe: 3.52
Socialist countries (except the USSR and China): 2.75
Middle East: 1.77
Latin America: 1.11
China: 0.74
Africa: 0.37
Asia (except Japan): 0.35
World population (1988): 5128 million

Population (millions). Each notched section represents 100 million.

Many of the countries which produce and use only a small amount of energy at the moment want to improve their living standards, but this would mean that they would greatly increase their energy use.

As you can see from the graph on the left, there were far more people using a small amount of energy in 1988 than there were using large amounts. If they all increased their energy use, the drain on the world's reserves would be enormous (and so would the increase in environmental damage). Below and at the top of page 91, there are some maps which show the state of the world's energy reserves.

World fossil fuel reserves

These special maps are based on the area groups on pages 88-89 (though in two cases, Australia and New Zealand are put together with Asia, because their figures are too small to single them out individually).

Most of the areas are in roughly the right geographical position, but their sizes are not their geographical sizes. The number of little squares each area occupies shows the known reserves of oil, gas and coal in that area in 1988. You can see how the Middle East dominates the oil map, the Middle East and the USSR dominate the gas map, and the USA, the USSR and China dominate the coal map.

Key to country groups

- North America
- Latin America
- Western Europe
- Middle East
- Africa
- Asia
- Australia and New Zealand
- Asia, Australia and New Zealand
- Socialist countries

Known oil reserves in billion barrels (1 square = 1 billion barrels)

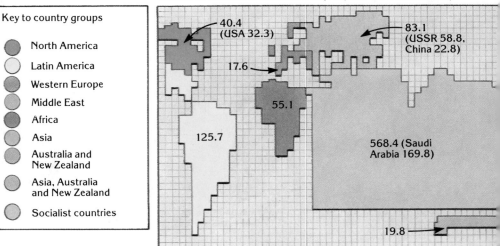

40.4 (USA 32.3)
83.1 (USSR 58.8, China 22.8)
17.6
55.1
125.7
568.4 (Saudi Arabia 169.8)
19.8

Known natural gas reserves in trillion cubic feet (1 square = 0.1 trillion cubic feet)

Known coal reserves in billion tons (1 square = 1 billion tons)

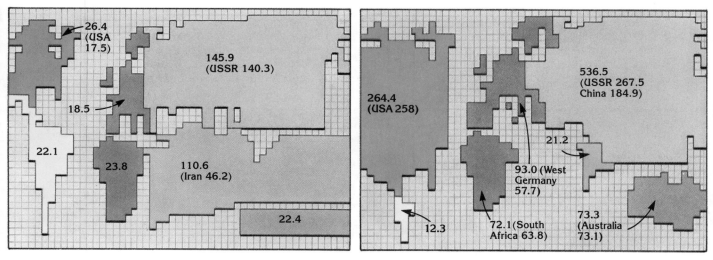

The graphs below show how long the reserves of each area would last, if they continued to be produced (brought out of the ground) at the same (average) rate as that area produced them in 1988 (see page 88). The figure for the whole world shows how long world reserves would last if we continued to produce oil, coal and gas at the average 1988 rate (the average of the rates of all the countries).

The danger is that we will continue to increase our demand for energy and, because of this, our rates of production. This would mean that the reserves would not even last as long as these graphs show.

Years of oil reserves remaining

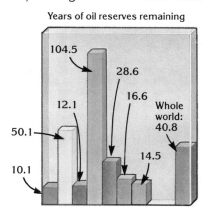

Years of gas reserves remaining

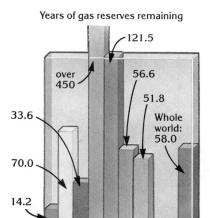

Years of coal reserves remaining (this graph has a different scale)

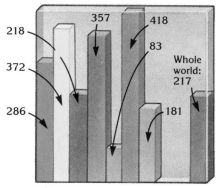

Although more oil, gas or coal may be discovered, we cannot rely on this. We must become much more energy efficient (use less energy in future years), so we can make the reserves last longer. In particular, the countries which use the most energy per head at the moment (see page 90) must drastically reduce their energy use, and help the poor countries build up their industries in the most energy-efficient way.

Another way we can secure enough energy in the future is to develop our use of renewable sources, such as the sun and the wind. This will also help to reduce the environmental damage caused by burning fossil fuels.

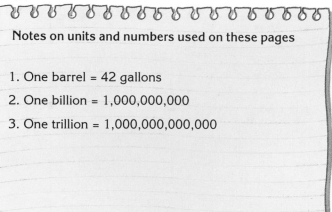

Notes on units and numbers used on these pages

1. One barrel = 42 gallons

2. One billion = 1,000,000,000

3. One trillion = 1,000,000,000,000

The economics of energy

There are many costs and benefits involved in the production of energy. Large amounts of money are spent when a power station is built, and also to keep it working. If the power station has been planned properly, though, this expenditure should be balanced, and exceeded, by the amount of money earned from selling the energy, and from other sideline benefits.

There are also hidden costs and benefits involved in producing energy, and these may be difficult to measure in terms of money. People are now becoming more aware of such things as pollution and noise disturbance, and it is important that these factors are also considered. Below you can see these factors included in an economic plan of a refuse-burning power station (see pages 76-77).

Energy is produced in a refuse-burning power station by burning household and commercial refuse (waste). This would otherwise simply be buried in large dumps, called landfill sites. An ideal, energy-efficient, refuse-burning power station would also be part of a CHP system (see page 82), so that the hot water it produces is not wasted.

Other costs (not normally considered)

Damage to the environment due to the release of gases (such as hydrogen chloride, carbon dioxide and sulphur dioxide), dust and particles of heavy metals (such as mercury and cadmium).

Disturbance to the local community, due to such things as noise, smells, soot and extra traffic.

Benefits (normally considered)

Money from selling electricity

Money from the local authority as a payment for taking away its refuse.

Money from selling metals and other materials extracted from the refuse.

Money from selling hot water (produced in the power station) as part of a CHP system (see page 84).

Costs (normally considered)

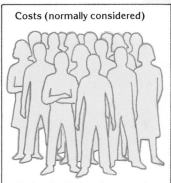

Paying the fees and wages of the architects, engineers and construction workers who designed and built the power station, and the management and workers who operate it.

Buying the land the power station is built on and the materials to build it with.

Buying basic supplies and paying for repairs and new machine parts needed to keep the power station running.

Paying for transportation to bring the refuse and other supplies to the power station, and take away the ash.

Other benefits (not normally considered)

The amount of refuse to be buried is reduced to a relatively small amount of ash. This means the landfill site(s) will last longer and transportation costs are lower because fewer trucks are needed.

There is less danger of pollution caused by poisonous substances seeping into local water from the landfill site(s).

Other costs, such as insurance, taxes and possibly interest payments (extra payments that must be made if money was borrowed to help start up the power station).

Up to now, the other, "extra" costs have almost always been ignored during planning, because they are difficult to assess. It is also particularly true of power stations burning fossil fuels that pollution is very much accepted as a fact, and is not seen as a cost. So, from this point of view, there are not really any other "extra" benefits which can be gained from operating in a different way.

To work out the economics of a truly "environment-friendly" power station, the extra costs should be included, as far as possible, in the figures. For example, the release of harmful substances could be greatly reduced by spending more money on anti-pollution devices. So the price of these devices should be put in the "costs" column. It is very important that people begin to plan in this way, so that the true cost of producing energy can be calculated.

Further information

Below are some addresses of organizations, groups and government offices which are concerned with energy resources and the production, consumption and conservation of energy. They will be able to provide you with further information.

If you want to find out about smaller, local groups that are concerned with energy issues, you could try asking at your local library or writing to the main offices of the organizations listed below, to see if they have local branches.

International

International Energy Agency
2, Rue Andre-Pascal
75775 Paris Cedex 16, France

International Atomic Energy
Authority
Wagramerstrasse 5
P.O. Box 100
A-1400 Vienna, Austria

Friends of the Earth International
26–28 Underwood Street
London N1 7JQ, England

Greenpeace International
Keizersgracht 176
1016 DW, Amsterdam
The Netherlands

United Kingdom

National Power
Sudbury House
15 Newgate Street
London EC1A 7AU

Powergen
53 New Broad Street
London EC2M 1JJ

Energy Efficiency Office
1 Palace Street
London SW1E 5HE

Association for the Conservation of
Energy
9 Sherlock Mews
London W1M 3RH

UK Atomic Energy Authority
11 King Charles II Street
London SW1Y 4QP

National Centre for Alternative
Technology
Machynlleth
Powys SY20 9AZ

United States of America

American Council for an Energy
Efficient Economy
1001 Connecticut Avenue NW
Washington, DC 20036

Electric Power Research Institute
3412 Hillview Avenue
P.O. Box 10412
Palo Alto,
California 94303

Solar Energy Research Institute
1617 Cole Boulevard
Golden,
Colorado 80401

World Resources Institute
1735 New York Avenue NW
Washington, DC 20006

World Watch Institute
1776 Massachusetts Avenue NW
Washington, DC 20036

Environmental Defense Fund
257 Park Avenue South
New York, NY 10010

Australia and New Zealand

Energy Information Centre
139 Flinders Street
Melbourne 3000
Victoria

Energy Planning Office
Energy Information Centre
222 North Terrace
Adelaide 5000
South Australia

State Energy Commission
465 Wellington Street
Perth 6000
Western Australia

Canada

Atomic Energy of Canada
344 Slater Street
Ottawa
Ontario K1A 0S4

Energy Resources Conservation
Board
640-5 Avenue SW
Calgary
Alberta T2P 3G4

Energy Probe Research Foundation
100 College Street
Toronto
Ontario M5G 1L5

Department of Energy, Mines and
Resources
580 Booth Street
Ottawa
Ontario K1A 0E4

Ontario Hydro
700 University Avenue
Toronto
Ontario M5G 1X6

Australian Conservation Federation
672B Glenferrie Road
Hawthorn 3122
Victoria

Victorian Solar Energy Council
10th Floor
270 Flinders Street
Melbourne 3000
Victoria

Ministry of Energy
P.O. Box 2337
Wellington
New Zealand

Glossary

Atoms. The "building blocks" of all substances. They are very tiny particles, each one made up of even tinier particles called **protons**, **neutrons** and **electrons**. The different amounts of these determine what substance the atom is.

Biogas. Gas produced by rotting material such as animal manure and other farm, household and industrial waste. The gas contains **methane** and can be used as a fuel to heat buildings or generate electricity.

Biomass. All types of organic (animal or plant) material. Biomass is a store of energy, which can be converted into other types of energy, e.g. wood, straw or manure can be burned to produce heat and light energy.

Chemical energy. Energy stored in a substance and released during a chemical reaction. Fuels such as wood, coal, oil and food all contain chemical energy. The reaction when they are burned (or digested) releases the energy, e.g. as heat and light energy.

Conductor. A material through which heat or an electric current can flow easily. Copper and iron are both good conductors.

Conservation of energy. When energy changes from one form to another (e.g. when fuel burns), the total amount of energy before the change is always the same as the total amount of energy after the change. The energy is always conserved. It cannot be destroyed.

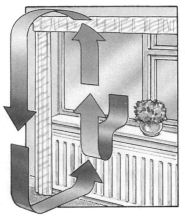

Convection. One way that heat travels through a liquid or gas. When heated, the **molecules** near the heat source gain more energy, moving faster and further apart. The heated liquid or gas then moves upwards, because it is now less dense and lighter. Cooler liquid or gas, with more densely-packed molecules, sinks to take its place.

Distillation. The process of separating a mixture of liquids by heating. The different liquids evaporate at different temperatures; the one with the lowest boiling point evaporates first. The separated gases are condensed back into liquids by cooling.

Dynamo. A machine which changes **kinetic energy** into electrical energy.

Electromagnetic energy. Energy which travels in waves, such as ultra-violet radiation. It can be thought of as a combination of electric and magnetic energy.

Electromagnetism. The effect whereby a magnetic field is produced around a wire when an electric current is passed through the wire. Electromagnets (see pages 71 and 72) use this principle.

Electromotive force. The force needed to drive an electric current in an electric circuit. It is measured in volts.

Electrons. Particles which form part of an **atom**. They move around its **nucleus**.

Fission. The splitting up of the **nucleus** of a heavy **atom** into two (or more) lighter nuclei. It releases huge amounts of energy.

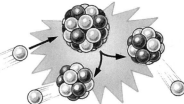

Fossil fuels. Fuels which result from the compression of the remains of living matter over millions of years. Coal, oil and natural gas are all fossil fuels.

Friction. The resistance between two touching surfaces (or one surface and the air) when they move over each other. This slows down the moving object(s). Some of the kinetic energy changes into other types of energy.

Fusion. The joining together (fusing) of the **nuclei** of two or more **atoms** into one heavier nucleus. It releases vast amounts of energy.

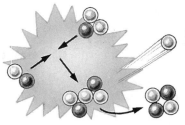

Generator. A device which turns **mechanical energy** into electricity. The mechanical energy may be provided by an engine or a **turbine**.

Geothermal energy. The heat energy which is produced by natural processes inside the earth. It can be extracted from hot springs, reservoirs of hot water deep below the ground or by breaking open the rock itself.

Greenhouse effect. The warming effect produced when radiation cannot escape to the atmosphere or space. A good example is what happens in a greenhouse (hence the name). Short-wave radiation from the sun penetrates the glass of the greenhouse, and is absorbed by the plants, but the long-wave radiation that the plants emit cannot get back out through the glass. Carbon dioxide and other gases in the atmosphere act like the greenhouse glass. The levels of these gases are increasing, so the climate is slowly getting warmer (called global warming).

Grid system. A network of cables which carry electricity from power stations, where it is produced, to the cities, towns and villages of a country.

Hydrocarbons. Chemical compounds which contain only carbon and hydrogen **atoms**. They are the dominant compounds in **fossil fuels**.

Hydro-electricity. Electricity which is produced from moving water. In a typical hydro-electric power station, the water turns **turbines**, which are attached to **generators**.

Insulator. A bad **conductor**, e.g. wood or plastic. These substances slow down the progress of electricity or heat energy.

Joule(J). The unit of measurement of energy, which is now commonly used in preference to the calorie (4.2kJ) One thousand joules equal one kilojoule (kJ). Because measured quantities are usually at least a thousand joules, kilojoules are normally used in measurements.

Kinetic energy. The energy of movement. The faster an object moves, the more kinetic energy it has. Also, the more mass a moving object has, the more kinetic energy it has.

Methane. A gas (a **hydrocarbon**) which is produced by organic (plant and animal) matter when it rots in the absence of oxygen. Natural gas is mainly methane.

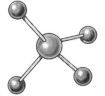

Molecules. Particles which normally consist of two or more **atoms** joined together, e.g. a water molecule is made up of two hydrogen atoms and one oxygen atom.

Neutrons. Particles which form part of the **nucleus** of an atom (**protons** make up the rest of the nucleus).

Nucleus (pl. **nuclei**). The central part of an **atom**, made up of tightly-packed **protons** and **neutrons**.

Photosynthesis. The process by which green plants make food (carbohydrates) from water and carbon dioxide, using the energy in sunlight. The food is a store of **chemical energy** inside the plants.

Photovoltaic cell. Another name for a **solar cell**.

Potential energy. Energy that is stored in an object due to its being within the influence of a force field, e.g. a magnetic or gravitational field.

Power. The rate at which energy is produced or used. It is generally stated as the rate of doing work or the rate of change of energy. Power is measured in watts (W). One watt equals one **joule** per second.

Protons. Particles which form part of the **nucleus** of an atom. The other particles in the nucleus are **neutrons**.

Radioactivity. A property of the **atoms** of certain substances, due to the fact that their **nuclei** are unstable. They give out energy in the form of particles or waves.

Reactor. Part of a nuclear power station – the structure inside which **fission** occurs in millions of atomic **nuclei**, producing vast amounts of heat energy.

Renewable energy. Energy from sources which are constantly available in the natural world, such as wind, water or the sun.

Solar cell. A device, usually made from silicon, which converts some of the energy in sunlight directly into electricity.

Turbine. A device with blades, which is turned by a force, e.g. that of wind, water or high pressure steam. The **kinetic energy** of the spinning turbine is converted into electricity in a **generator**.

Index

Acid rain, 65, 86, 87
Active solar heating, 74
Appliances (household), 53, 83
Atoms, 56, 58, 94

Batteries, 57, 79
Biogas, 77, 94
Biomass, 76, 94
Butane, 67

Cars, 55, 85, 86
Charcoal, 76
Chemical energy, 52, 54, 55, 56, 57, 63, 94
CHP (combined heat and power), 83, 84
Coal, 56, 63, 64-65, 88, 89, 91
    -mining, 64-65
Conduction (heat/electricity), 59, 60
Conductors, 59, 60, 94
Conservation of energy, 54, 94
Convection, 59, 94
Current (electric), 60

Dams, 80-81
Distillation, 66, 94
Dynamo, 70, 94

Electrical energy/electricity, 54, 57, 60,
    61, 70-71, 74, 76, 79, 80, 81
Electromagnetic energy, 54, 61, 62, 94
Electromagnetic spectrum, 61
Electromagnetism, 94
Electromagnets, 70, 71, 72
Electromotive force, 60, 94
Electrons, 56, 94
Embedded energy, 84
Energy chains, 55, 76
Energy economics, 92
Energy efficiency, 55
    in the home, 82-83
    in industry, 84
    in transportation, 85
Ethane, 67

Fission, 57, 68, 94
Fossil fuels, 63, 64-67, 70, 88, 89, 90,
    91, 94
Fractionating column, 66
Fractions, 66
Friction, 55, 94
Fuels, 56
Fusion, 57, 62, 68, 94

Gamma rays, 61
Gas (natural), 56, 63, 66-67, 88, 89, 91
Generator, 70, 94
    turbine-, 68, 70-71, 76, 79, 80, 81
Geothermal energy (underground heat),
    63, 81, 94
Gravitational potential energy, 57, 58
Greenhouse effect, 65, 86, 95
Grid system, 71, 79, 95

Heat energy, 54, 56, 58-59, 63
Heat wheel, 84
Hydrocarbons, 66, 67, 95
Hydro-electricity/hydro-electric power,
    63, 80-81, 89, 95

Infra-red radiation, 59, 61, 62
Insulators (heat/electricity), 59, 60, 95

Joules, 53, 95

Kinetic energy, 52, 54, 55, 58, 59, 95

Landfill sites, 67, 92
Light energy, 54, 55, 61

Magnetic energy/magnetism, 61
Magnetic potential energy, 57
Mechanical energy, 58, 59, 70
Methane, 67, 77, 95
Microwaves, 61
Molecules, 56, 58, 95

Neutrons, 57, 95
Nuclear energy/power, 54, 57, 68-69, 89
Nuclear fuel, 69
Nuclear reactors, 68, 95
Nucleus, 56, 57, 95

Oil, 56, 63, 66-67, 87, 88, 89, 90, 91
    -refining, 66-67
OTEC, 81

Passive solar heating, 73
Photosynthesis, 63, 95
Photovoltaic cells, see Solar cells
Plants (used for energy) 63, 76-77
Pollution, 56, 65, 67, 73, 77, 85, 86, 87, 92
Potential energy, 54, 57, 95
Power, 53, 95
Power stations, 61, 68-69, 70-71, 76-77,
    83, 84
Primary energy consumption, 89, 90
Propane, 67
Protons, 56, 95
Public transportation, 85

Quality of energy, 61

Radar, 61
Radiation
    (process), 59
    infra-red-, 59, 61, 62
    ultra-violet-, 61, 62
    (result of radioactivity), 69
Radioactive waste, 69
Radioactivity, 69, 95
Radio waves, 61
Reactors (nuclear), 68, 95
Refuse (burned for energy), 76-77, 92
Renewable energy, 73, 95

Solar energy, 62, 63, 73-75
Solar cells, 74, 95
Solar collectors, 74
Solar heating, 73-74
Sound energy, 54, 59
Static electricity, 60
Stored energy, 52, 56-57
Strain energy, 52, 55, 57

Temperature, 58
Tidal barrage, 80
Tidal energy, 63, 80
Tides, 63
Town gas, 67
Transformers, 71
Transportation, 85
Turbine, 70, 95
Turbine generators, 68, 70-71, 76, 79,
    80, 81

Ultra-violet radiation, 61, 62

Visible light, 61
Voltage/volts, 60, 71

Waste (radioactive), 69
Waste matter (used for energy), 76-77
Water cycle, 62-63
Water (used for energy), 62-63, 80-81
Watts, 53
Wave energy/power, 62, 63, 80
Wind, 60
Wind energy, 62, 78-79
Wind pump, 78
Wind turbines, 79
Wood (used for energy), 76, 77

X-rays, 61

We are grateful to "Green Teacher,"
Machynlleth, Powys, Wales, for
permission to use adaptations of
material previously published by
themselves (projects on pages 73, 75, 78
and 81).

The figures on pages 88-91 are based on
those given in the BP Statistical Review of
World Energy (July 1989), produced by
The British Petroleum Company plc,
Britannic House, Moor Lane, London
EC2Y 9BU, England, and the World
Population Data Sheet, produced by
Population Concern, 231 Tottenham
Court Road, London W1P 9AE, England.
We are grateful for permission to use
these statistics.